플라워 컬러 가이드
(Flower Color Guide)

뉴욕 플라워 스튜디오 퍼트남 & 퍼트남의 테일러와 마이클은

놀랍도록 창의적인 조합으로 추억의 색조를 구현하여 로맨틱하고 드라마틱한 플로럴 어렌지먼트와 인스톨레이션으로 명성을 쌓았다.

색은 그들의 플로럴 철학의 중심이자 창작 과정의 가장 중요한 요소이다. 이 책은 색상별로 정리된 절화 가이드북이다. 꽃 하나하나를 소개하는 동시에 독자 스스로 무수한 플로럴 조합을 시도해 볼 수 있도록 영감을 준다. 또한 독자는 각기 다른 색상의 두 가지 꽃으로 색의 점진적인 변화 과정을 보여주는 퍼트남 & 퍼트남의 '색 중심' 어렌지먼트 방식도 사용해 볼 수 있다.
이 책은 꽃의 색감, 계절별로 유용한 꽃, 꽃의 특징에 대한 정보를 보기 쉽게 담고 있어 독자들이 다양한 형태와 크기의 꽃들을 사용하여 더욱 아름다운 어렌지먼트를 만들 수 있도록 도와줄 것이다.

'플라워 컬러 가이드'는 아름다운 사진뿐만 아니라 꽃 관리법, 계절에 따른 시장 출하 여부, 환경을 고려한 지속 가능성과 같은 유용한 정보를 담고 있다. 이 책은 전문 플로리스트와 이벤트 플래너뿐만 아니라 식물에 대한 열정과 무궁무진한 색상 조합에 강한 흥미를 가진 사람 모두에게 완벽한 책이라 하겠다.

테일러와 마이클 퍼트남은

2014년 뉴욕에 그들의 플라워 스튜디오 퍼트남 & 퍼트남을 오픈함과 동시에 각종 패션쇼, 웨딩, 꽃장식, 파티, 화보 촬영을 위해 찾아야 하는 중요 플로리스트로 등극했다.
꽃으로 만들어내는 자연스럽고 우아한 색감의 조합은 네덜란드 정물화의 풍요로움을 환기시키는 독자적인 그들의 미학을 담고 있다.

그들의 작업은 더블유 매거진, 하퍼스 바자, 엘르 데코, 보그에 특집으로 실렸다. 그리고 디올, 까르띠에, 아담 리페스, 제이슨 우, 브랜든 맥스웰 등 여러 브랜드와 협업했다.

플라워 컬러 가이드
(Flower Color Guide)

테일러 & 마이클 퍼트남 저
김정용 역 이주희 감수

아트앤아트피플

일러두기 '플라워 컬러 가이드'에 소개된 꽃들의 한국명은 시장에서 통용되는 이름 중심으로 표기되었다. 한국 꽃시장에서는 꽃이름으로 보통명(common name)또는 식물학명(botanical name) 중 하나를 사용하는 경우가 많다. 대부분의 꽃도감은 순수 우리말 또는 학명을 꽃이름(e.g. 노루오줌 꽃/아스틸베)으로 사용한다. 하지만 독자들이 이 책을 실생활에서 더욱 적극적으로 사용할 수 있기를 바라며, 한국 꽃시장에서 통용되는 이름으로 정리했음을 밝힌다. 이 책에 소개된 꽃자재 이름과 꽃 관리법 역시 동일한 이유로 꽃시장 또는 전문가들이 사용하는 이름으로 표기했다.

번역 김정용은 경북대학교에서 인류학, 고고학, 국문학을 공부했다. 지금은 캐나다에서 다양한 언어와 문화를 배우고 있다. 옮긴 책으로《디지털시대, 책 읽는 아이로 키우기》《나는 고양이 푸쉰》《마법의 유니콘 협회 공식입문서》가 있다.

감수 이주희(플로리스트, 이에나 대표)는 고려대학교에서 영문학, 동대학원에서 국제학을 공부했다. 이후 영국으로 유학, 맥퀸즈에서 플라워 디자인 과정을 수료하고 파리로 넘어가 카트린 뮐러에서 통번역을 겸하며 플로리스트로 일했다. 지금은 한옥 플라워 아뜰리에, 이에나에서 꽃을 만들고 가르치며, 다양한 행사를 기획하고 있다.

FLOWER COLOR GUIDE © 2018 Taylor Putnam and Michael Putnam
Originally published by Phaidon Press Limited All rights reserved. No part of this publication may be reproduced, stored in a retrieval system or transmitted, in any form or by any means, electronic, mechanical, photocopying, recording or otherwise, without the prior permission of Phaidon Press.

This Korean edition was published by ARTNARTPEOPLE in 2025 under licence from Phaidon Press Limited, of 2 Cooperage Yard, London, E15 2QR, UK arranged through Hobak Agency, South Korea.

이 책은 호박 에이전시(Hobak Agency)를 통한 저작권자와의 독점계약으로 아트앤아트피플에서 출간되었습니다. 저작권법에 의해 한국 내에서 보호를 받는 저작물이므로 무단전재와 복제를 금합니다.

색	6
꽃	15
부록	417
꽃을 구매하기 전	419
꽃 관리의 기본	421
필수 도구	425
화병 준비하기	429
추천 컬러 팔레트	433
환경을 고려한 지속 가능성에 관하여	435
절취 가능한 꽃 사진	437
식물학명 색인	477
보통명 색인	481

색

색은 꽃꽂이를 하거나 대규모 화훼 장식물을 설치할 때, 퍼트남 & 퍼트남의 작업을 정의하는 가장 중요한 특징이다. 우리는 색을 사랑하고, 색을 통해 시각적으로 가장 멋진 이야기를 만들어낼 수 있다고 생각한다.

우리는 직관적인 플로럴 디자인을 한다. 색은 하나의 이야기이다. 우리는 꽃의 색채가 이끄는 대로 따라가며 색을 쌓아 올리는 과정을 통해 깊이감을 더한다. 또한 오래된 골동품과 같은 색부터 강렬하고 선명한 색까지, 모든 색을 아우르며 사용한다. 자연스럽고 고풍스러운 느낌을 주기 위해 우리는 절화(花)와 절지(草)뿐만 아니라 과일, 덩굴 등과 같은 다른 여러 요소들도 꽃꽂이에 적극 활용한다. 하지만 우리는 절지보다는 절화에 더 큰 비중을 두고 작업한다.

남부 캘리포니아에서 어린 시절을 보낸 마이클은 꽃과 정원의 아름다움을 가까이에서 접하고 자란 영향으로, 색감을 보는 매우 세련된 안목을 갖게 되었다. 이후 인테리어 디자인 공부를 하고 그 분야에서 일하게 되면서 그의 심미안은 한층 깊어졌다. 또한 테일러는 사진작가로서의 풍부한 경험을 통해 색에 대한 이해를 완성했다.

우리는 색을 염두에 두고 디자인을 시작한다. 이른 아침, 우리는 현재 거주하고 있는 뉴욕 웨스트 28번가 꽃시장으로 향한다. 그리고 우리가 말하고자 하는 색의 이야기를 가진 모든 꽃들을 찾기 위해 시장의 꽃들을 하나하나 살펴본다. 색에 대한 생각은 항상 우리를 이끌고 우리에게 영감을 준다. 그리고 이 책은 2014년 퍼트남 & 퍼트남을 시작했을 때 우리가 그토록 찾길 원했던 안내서라 말하고 싶다.

이 책은 꽃의 유형, 꽃이 가지고 있는 색의 스펙트럼, 꽃의 계절별 구입시기와 구입가능 여부가 잘 정리된 쉽고 실용적인 참고서이다. 집을 꽃으로 장식하고 싶을 때, 선물할 꽃을 만들 때, 디너파티 또는 웨딩 준비를 할 때, 이 책을 꽃꽂이와 꽃 품종 선택을 위한 필수 입문서로 활용하길 바란다.

우리는 제철에 구할 수 있는 꽃의 사용을 강조한다. 오늘날 우리는 다양한 꽃들을 언제 어디서나 쉽게 구할 수 있다. 글로벌해진 꽃시장은 사계절 내내 세계 각국에서 수입된 꽃들로 채워지고, 그 꽃들의 대부분은 네덜란드를 거쳐 유통된다. 우리의 주된 목표는 가까운 곳에서 구할 수 있는 가장 신선하고 매력적이며 아름다운 꽃을 사용하는 것이다. 이 책을 읽는 독자들 역시 마찬가지일 것이다. 가까운 곳에서 재배된 꽃을 사용하면 탄소 배출량을 줄이는 부가적인 효과도 얻을 수 있다. 사실 가장 아름다운 꽃은 계절마다 집 주변에서 활짝 피는 제철의 꽃들이다. 그 꽃들은 제철에 가장 아름다운 모습으로 피어 있을 뿐만 아니라 장거리 운송을 통해 유통된 꽃이 아니기에 더욱 저렴한 가격에 판매되며, 심지어 훨씬 더 오래간다.

초보 플로리스트들이 직면하는 문제는 대부분의 사람들이 꽃에 대해 잘 알지 못한다는 사실이다. 우리 역시 마찬가지였다. 상담을 위해 찾아온 고객들은 언제나 "꽃의 이름은 잘 모르지만 제가 좋아하는 꽃은 …." 이라고 말한다. 대부분의 고객은 주로 결혼을 준비하는 신부들인데 그들이 말하는 꽃은 대개 작약이나 가든 장미이다. "전 핑크색 꽃을 좋아해요." 라고 말하는 고객도 있다. 물론 다른 색을 말할 때도 있지만 결국에는 " 그런데 그 꽃이 무슨 종류인지는 몰라요." 라는 말을 듣게 된다.

퍼트남 & 퍼트남의 이름으로 사업이 성장하면서 우리는 사람들이 단지 꽃꽂이를 하는 방법뿐만 아니라 꽃에 대해서도 배우고 싶어한다는 것을 알게 되었다. 그리고 꽃을 배우고자 하는 사람들의 열정만큼이나 우리도 우리가 알고 있는 지식을 그들과 나누고 싶은 마음이 커졌다. 요리의 경우, 식자재에 대해 배우고, 여러 재료들이 어떻게 어우러지는지 알면, 요리 준비 과정을 더욱 즐길 수 있게 되는 것은 물론, 요리 실력도 자연스레 늘게 된다. 꽃도 마찬가지다. 꽃에 대해 알면 알수록 꽃 사용에 있어서의 경험과 지식은 확장되며, 시간과 경험이 쌓일수록 꽃의 응용 능력은 향상된다. 소비자의 입장에서도, 꽃에 대해 많이 알고 있으면 꽃을 구매할 때나 플로리스트에게 의뢰할 때 분명 도움이 될 것이다.

꽃꽂이의 역사는 대중의 인기를 반영하는 유행과 양식의 변화라 할 수 있다. 우리는 짙은 색과 바랜 듯한 색을 사용하여 라인감과 질감을 표현하고, 넘쳐흐르거나 탁자 위로 흩어져 내리는 것들을 표현함으로써 낭만적이고 자유로운 감성을 끌어내는 것을 좋아한다.

우리가 무엇보다 주안점을 두는 것은 색의 그러데이션이다. 변색 또는 혼색의 과정을 충분히 거치지 않아 보기에 과하고 부자연스러운 물방울무늬(polka-dot)방식의 배열과는 아주 다른 방식이다. 색상 사이사이에 존재하는 색들을 인지하게 되면 한층 격상된 플라워 디자인을 할 수 있게 된다. 우리는 전 세계를 돌며 꽃꽂이 워크샵을 진행하고 있다. 꽃꽂이 워크샵은 우리가 가장 좋아하는 일 중 하나인데, 우리는 이 수업에서 색의 그러데이션을 학생들에게 이해시키는 데 집중한다. 수업은 스펙트럼 안의 서로 다른 색을 가진 두 줄기의 꽃으로 시작하여 그 색과 어우러지는 다른 색의 꽃들을 더해가며 진행된다. 이 방법으로 작업을 하다 보면 기존의 색이 다른 색과 어울려 완전히 다른 색으로 변한다. 이러한 일련의 과정을 보는 것은 매우 흥미롭다.

각각의 꽃들은 각기 다른 특색을 어렌지먼트에 부여한다. 우리는 꽃이 가진 각기 다른 특색들이 서로 균형을 이루는 것이 중요하다고 생각한다. 우리는 꽃을 네 그룹으로 구분한다. 형태 꽃(face flowers), 질감 꽃 (textural flowers), 라인 꽃(gestural stems) 그리고 채우는 꽃(fillers)이다. 아마릴리스(amaryllis), 작약 (peonies), 달리아(dahlias) 와 같은 꽃들은 형태 꽃(face flowers)에 해당되는데, 이 꽃들은 어렌지먼트의 중심이 되거나 이목을 집중시키는 역할을 한다. 질감 꽃(textural flowers)에는 아스틸베(astilbe), 왁스 플라워(wax flower), 안드로메다(andromeda)와 같은 꽃들이 있는데, 이 꽃들은 어렌지먼트에 흥미를 더하는 역할을 한다. 디기탈리스(foxgloves), 프리틸라리아(fritillaria), 튤립(tulips) 같은 라인 꽃들(gestural stems)은 형태나 모양을 만들고 어렌지먼트에 깊이감과 생동감을 부여한다. 마지막으로 장미, 리시안셔스(lisianthus), 카네이션과 같은 채우는 꽃들(fillers)은 색을 혼합하고 기본 토대를 만드는데 활용한다.

이 책을 활용하는 가장 좋은 방법을 소개하겠다. 일단, 당신이 가장 좋아하는 색으로 시작하길 권한다. 색이 정해지면 그 색이 있는 페이지를 찾아 당신이 원하는 시기에 어떤 꽃들을 구할 수 있는지 확인하라. 사람들은 꽃의 종류나 색을 특정 짓는 것을 매우 좋아한다. 우리는 당신이 이 책을 읽는 동안, 이전에는 한번도 생각지 못한 꽃의 색감과 꽃의 종류를 발견하길 바란다. 그리고 더 나아가 어떤 색들이 서로 잘 어울리는지에 대한 우리의 제안을 참고하여 꽃의 색과 종류에 대한 탐구를 이어 나가길 바란다.

준비 과정은 성공적인 꽃꽂이의 핵심이다. 플라워 샵이나 꽃시장에 가기 전, 당신이 원하는 이미지를 생각해 두는 것이 좋다. 어떤 목적으로 꽃을 구입하는지를 생각해 보라. 결혼식을 위한 꽃인가? 생일이나 디너 파티를 위한 꽃인가? 또는 혼자 보고 즐길 수 있는 집안 장식용 꽃인가? 계절도 고려해야 한다. 지역에서 재배되는 제철의 꽃이 가장 싱싱하고 가격도 좋을 뿐 아니라 꽃의 수명도 길다. 꽃은 꽃송이 그 자체만 중요한 것이 아니라는 사실도 기억하자. 꽃의 줄기와 잎 또한 아름다운 선을 지니고 있고, 모든 꽃들은 고유의 움직임을 가지고 있다.

처음에는 책 내용을 계절별로 정리하려고 했다. 그러다가 꽃 종류와 이름을 알파벳순으로 정리하는 것이 더 낫겠다고 생각했다. 하지만 최종적으로 우리는 이 책을 색 중심으로 정리하기로 결정했다. 사람들이 꽃을 생각할 때, 본능적으로 색을 가장 먼저 떠올리기 때문이다. 이 책에서 당신은 흰색, 크림색, 연한 파스텔과 같이 밝은 색의 꽃부터, 어두운 보라, 갈색, 검정에 가까운 어두운 색까지, 단계별로 정리된 색감의 꽃들을 만나게 될 것이다.

이 책에는 400종의 꽃이 담겨 있다. 이 책에 담길 꽃을 선택하는 과정은 하나의 모험이자 창의적 시도였다는 사실을 당신이 알아주기를 바란다. 세상엔 각양각색, 천차만별의 꽃들이 존재한다. 심지어 400종의 튤립만으로 책을 만들 수 있을 정도이다. 당신이 좋아하는 꽃도 이 책 안에 담겨 있기를 바란다. 우리는 가장 아름답고 다양한 색의 범위를 찾기 위해 가을부터 시작해, 이듬해 봄, 여름까지 총 일 년간 사진 촬영을 진행했다.

우리는 2008년 남부 캘리포니아의 식료품 가게 계산대 줄에서 처음 만났다. 테일러는 사진을, 마이클은 인테리어 디자인을 공부하는 대학생이었다. 우리의 인연은 그렇게 시작되었고, 만난 순간부터 언젠가는 둘이 함께 일하고 싶다고 생각했다. 단지 그때는 어떤 일로 우리가 함께 일하게 될지 몰랐을 뿐이었다.

마이클이 뉴욕 패션기술대학교(Fashion Institute of Technology. 이하 FIT)에 입학 허가를 받고 우리는 뉴욕으로 떠났다. 테일러는 사진을 보정하는 일을 하면서 주말에는 사진작가로서 경력을 쌓았다. FIT 졸업 후, 마이클은 디자인 회사에 취직했지만 손으로 작업하길 좋아하는 그가 충분히 만족할 만한 일은 아니었다. 그래서 그는 취미삼아 주말마다 지역 공원과 꽃시장에서 꽃을 구매하여 꽃꽂이를 하기 시작했다. 테일러는 마이클이 만든 꽃을 작은 정물화처럼 찍어 인스타그램에 올렸다. 그 사진들은 곧 사람들의 이목을 끌었고 마이클에게는 친구 선물용 꽃, 디너 파티, 브라이덜 샤워와 같은 소소한 꽃 작업 의뢰가 들어오기 시작했다. 그러던 어느 날, 보그 매거진에서 마이클에게 연락을 취해왔다. 그들은 마이클에게 기획 기사를 위한 꽃 작업을 의뢰했고, 그 이후 모든 것이 달라지기 시작했다. 보그 매거진의 웹사이트에 마이클의 작업이 담긴 기사가 실린 후, 일은 눈덩이처럼 불어나기 시작했다.

얼마 되지 않아 우리에겐 본업을 그만 두어도 될 만큼 충분한 일감이 생겼다. 우리는 맨하튼으로 옮겨 퍼트남 & 퍼트남을 시작했다. 처음에는 이스트 사이드에 있는 작은 아파트에서 시작했지만 현재는 뉴욕의 꽃 중심지인 웨스트 28 번가에 자리를 잡았다.

퍼트남 & 퍼트남이 성장하고 발전하는 동안 우리는 일을 하며 접했던 꽃들에 대해 더욱더 깊이 알게 되었다. 우리는 잘 모르던 아름다운 꽃들을 발견했으며 또 각각의 꽃들이 가진 창의적인 잠재력에 매료되었다.

콘스탄스 스프라이는 꽃꽂이에 대해 이렇게 말했다. "당신의 뜻대로 만들어라. 당신의 별을 따라라. 독창적이고 싶다면 그렇게 하고 그렇게 하고 싶지 않다면 그리 하지 않아도 좋다. 그저 편하게, 자연스럽게, 예쁘게, 단순하게, 넘실넘실하게, 바로크 스타일로, 꾸밈없게, 말갛게, 정형화된 스타일로, 거칠게, 사랑스럽게, 전통적으로…, 그리고 배우고, 배우고 또 배워라. 눈을 크게 뜨고 모든 형태의 아름다움을 받아들여라."

책 사용 설명서

꽃 사진 옆에 적힌 설명을 참조하라. 이 설명을 통해 꽃 이름과 이용 형태에 따른 꽃의 분류 그리고 그 꽃이 어느 계절에 가장 좋은 상태로 시장에 출하되는지를 알 수 있다.

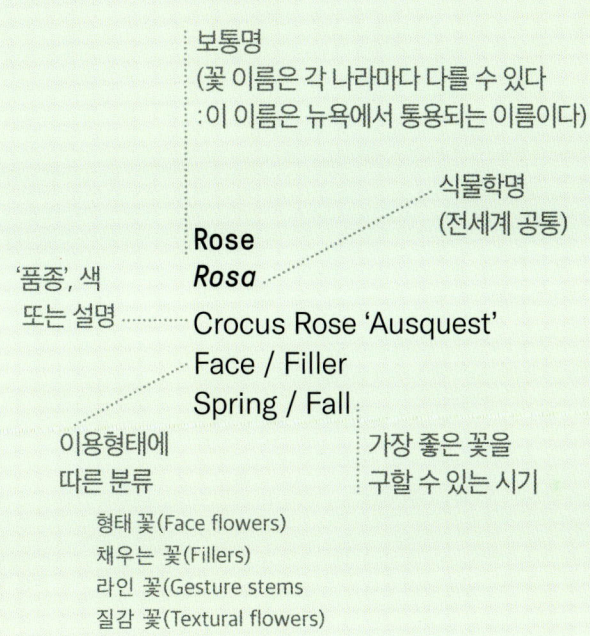

Notes

Notes

꽃

진달래 Azalea

Rhododendron molle

White
Filler
Spring

시클라멘 Cyclamen

Cyclamen persicum

White
Filler
Spring

수국 Hydrangea

Hydrangea macrophylla

White
Filler
Year-round

옥시페탈룸 Tweedia

Tweedia caerulea

'Pint White'
Filler
Year-round

벚나무 Flowering cherry

Prunus x subhirtella

'Autumnalis' white
Gesture / Filler
Spring

캥거루 발톱 Kangaroo paw
Anigozanthos

'Bush Diamond'
Gesture / Texture
Year-round

스톡 Stock
Matthiola incana
Double white
Gesture / Filler
Year-round

라넌큘러스 Ranunculus

Ranunculus asiaticus

Double white
Face / Filler
Winter / Spring

플란넬 플라워 Flannel flower
Actinotus helianthi

White
Filler / Texture
Winter / Spring

델피니움 Delphinium
Delphinium

'Centurion White'
Face / Gesture
Year-round

수선화 Paper white
Narcissus papyraceus

White
Filler
Winter / Spring

장미 Rose
Rosa
'Tibet'
Filler
Year-round

코와니 Allium / Naples onion
Allium neapolitanum
White
Gesture / Texture
Spring / Summer

백합 Lily

Lilium

'Premium Blond'
Face
Year-round

스프레이 카네이션 Spray carnation

Dianthus

'Grenadin White'
Texture / Filler
Year-round

스카비오사 Scabiosa

Scabiosa columbaria

White
Gesture
Year-round

네리네 Nerine
Nerine bowdenii
'Pallida' white
Filler / Texture
Year-round

아네모네 Anemone

Anemone coronaria

Single white
Face
Winter / Spring

조팝나무 Spirea

Spiraea

'Arguta'
Gesture / Texture
Winter / Spring

아네모네 Anemone

Anemone

De Caen Group white
Face
Winter / Spring

장미 Rose
Rosa

Winchester Cathedral 'Auscat'
Face / Filler
Spring / Fall

장미 Rose
Rosa
'White Majolica'
Filler
Year-round

스프레이 카네이션 Spray carnation

Dianthus

'Star Snow Tessino'
Filler / Texture
Year-round

작약 Peony

Paeonia

'Bowl of Cream'
Face
Spring

아마릴리스 Amaryllis

Hippeastrum

'White Dazzler'
Face
Winter

칼라 Calla lily
Zantedeschia aethiopica
White
Face / Gesture
Year-round

아스트란시아 Astrantia

Astrantia major

'White Giant'
Texture / Filler
Year-round

라일락 Lilac
Syringa vulgaris
White
Filler
Spring

달리아 Dahlia
Dahlia
'Blizzard'
Face
Summer / Fall

글라디올러스 Gladiolus
Gladiolus x colvillii
'Albus'
Gesture
Summer / Fall

글라디올러스 Gladiolus
Gladiolus

'White Prosperity'
Gesture
Year-round

프리지아 Freesia

Freesia

White
Filler
Year-round

수선화 Narcissus

Narcissus poeticus hybrid

White
Face / Filler
Winter / Spring

튤립 Tulip
Tulipa
'White Liberstar'
Gesture
Spring

히아신스 Hyacinth

Hyacinthus orientalis

White
Filler
Winter / Spring

장미 Rose
Rosa
'Garden Snow'
Filler
Year-round

은방울꽃 Lily of the valley
Convallaria majalis

White
Texture
Spring

둥글레 Solomon's Seal
Polygonatum biflorum

White
Gesture
Spring

무스카리 Muscari

Muscari azureum

'Album'
Texture / Filler
Winter / Spring

리시마치아 Gooseneck loosestrife
Lysimachia clethroides
White
Gesture
Summer

리시안셔스 Lisianthus

Eustoma russellianum

White
Filler
Year-round

거베라 Gerbera daisy
Gerbera x hybrida
White
Face / Gesture
Year-round

스위트피 Sweet pea
Lathyrus odoratus

White
Texture / Filler / Gesture
Winter / Spring

스노플레이크 Snowflake

Leucojum aestivum

White
Texture
Winter

스위트피 Everlasting pea
Lathyrus latifolius
'Albus' white
Texture / Filler / Gesture
Winter / Spring

아스틸베 Astilbe

Astilbe

'Deutschland'
Texture
Year-round

글라디올러스 Gladiolus
Gladiolus

'The Bride'
Gesture / Filler
Summer

튤립 Tulip

Tulipa

'Honeymoon'
Gesture
Spring

칼라 Calla lily

Zantedeschia

'Aspen'
Gesture
Year-round

안수리움 Anthurium

Anthurium

'Acropolis'
Face
Year-round

달리아 Dahlia
Dahlia

'Figaro' white
Face
Summer / Fall

코스모스 Cosmos

Cosmos bipinnatus

Double white
Gesture
Summer

니겔라 Nigella

Nigella damascena

White
Texture
Spring / Summer

디디스쿠스 Blue lace flower
Trachymene coerulea

'Lacy Pink'
Gesture
Spring / Summer

작약 Peony
Paeonia lactiflora
'Festiva Maxima'
Face
Spring

안수리움 Anthurium

Anthurium

'Lumina'
Face
Year-round

산당화 Quince
Chaenomeles speciosa
'Nivalis' white
Gesture
Winter

왁스 플라워 Wax flower

Chamelaucium uncinatum

White
Texture / Filler
Year-round

라이스플라워 Heath rice flower

Pimelea phylicoides

White
Texture
Spring / Summer

조팝나무 Spirea

Spiraea thunbergii

White
Gesture / Texture
Winter / Spring

작약 Peony

Paeonia lactiflora

'Sonata'
Face
Spring

작약 Peony
Paeonia lactiflora
'Rooster Reveille'
Face
Spring

스위트피 Sweet pea
Lathyrus odoratus

Pale pink
Texture / Filler / Gesture
Winter / Spring

작약 Peony

Paeonia lactiflora

'Duchesse de Nemours'
Face
Spring

버터플라이 라넌큘러스 Butterfly ranunculus
Ranunculus asiaticus

'Butterfly Lux' cream
Gesture / Filler
Winter / Spring

온시디움 Oncidium orchid
Oncidium hybrid
White and pink
Texture / Gesture
Year-round

산딸나무 Dogwood
Cornus kousa
var. chinensis
Gesture / Filler
Spring

디기탈리스 Foxglove
Digitalis purpurea
f. albiflora
Gesture / Face
Spring / Summer

장미 Rose
Rosa
'Champagne'
Filler
Year-round

장미 Rose
Rosa
'Charity'
Filler
Spring / Fall

재스민 Jasmine
Jasminum polyanthum
White and pink
Texture
Winter / Spring

수선화 Narcissus

Narcissus

'Salome'
Face / Filler
Spring

백합 Lily
Lilium

Pink roselily
Face
Year-round

스톡 Stock
Matthiola incana

Double peach
Filler / Gesture
Year-round

아스틸베 Astilbe

Astilbe

'Elizabeth Bloom'
Texture
Year-round

히아신스 Hyacinth

Hyacinthus orientalis

Pale pink
Filler
Winter / Spring

달리아 Dahlia
Dahlia
'Cream and Pink'
Face
Summer / Fall

국화 Chrysanthemum

Chrysanthemum

'Seaton's Je Dore'
Face
Fall

에피덴드룸 Epidendrum
Epidendrum hybrid
Pale pink
Gesture
Year-round

장미 Rose
Rosa
'Sahara'
Filler
Year-round

튤립 Tulip

Tulipa

'Apricot Beauty'
Gesture
Spring

독일붓꽃 Bearded iris
Iris germanica
'Party Dress'
Face
Spring

스타티스 Statice
Limonium sinuatum

Peach
Texture
Year-round

팬지 Pansy

Viola hybrid

Pale pink and yellow
Filler
Winter / Spring

장미 Rose
Rosa
'Cappuccino'
Filler
Year-round

스톡 Stock
Matthiola incana

Single petal peach
Gesture / Filler
Year-round

장미 Rose

Rosa

'Sahara Sensation'
Filler
Year-round

카네이션 Carnation

Dianthus

Nude
Filler
Year-round

달리아 Dahlia
Dahlia
'Cafe au Lait'
Face
Summer / Fall

장미 Rose
Rosa

Juliet 'Ausjameson'
Face / Filler
Year-round

리시안셔스 Lisianthus

Eustoma russellianum

Peach
Filler
Year-round

백합 Lily
Lilium

Peach
Face
Year-round

장미 Rose
Rosa
'Emily'
Filler
Year-round

장미 Rose
Rosa

'Pink Majolica'
Filler
Year-round

산딸나무 Dogwood
Cornus kousa
Pink
Gesture / Filler
Spring

모란 Tree peony

Paeonia x suffruticosa

'Kopper Kettle'
Face
Spring

장미 Rose
Rosa
'Distant Drum'
Face / Filler
Sping / Fall

거베라 Gerbera daisy

Gerbera x hybrida

Apricot
Face / Gesture
Year-round

라넌큘러스 Ranunculus
Ranunculua asiaticus

Double peach
Face / Filler
Winter / Spring

장미 Rose

Rosa

Pink-peach
Face / Filler
Spring / Fall

호접란 Phalaenopsis orchid
Phalaenopsis hybrid

Pale yellow and pink
Face / Filler / Gesture
Year-round

패롯 튤립 Parrot tulip

Tulipa

'Libretto Parrot'
Gesture
Spring

장미 Rose
Rosa
'Quicksand'
Filler
Year-round

칼라 Calla lily
Zantedeschia

'Kiwi Blush'
Gesture
Year-round

라넌큘러스 Ranunculus
Ranunculus asiaticus

Double pink
Face / Filler
Winter / Spring

디기탈리스 Foxglove
Digitalis purpurea

Pale pink
Gesture / Face
Spring / Summer

장미 Rose
Rosa
'Secret Garden'
Filler
Year-round

작약 Peony
Paeonia lactiflora
'Lady Gay'
Face
Spring

장미 Rose
Rosa

'Pink Raddish'
Texture / Filler
Year-round

카네이션 Carnation

Dianthus

Variegated
Filler
Year-round

장미 Rose
Rosa
'Caffe Latte'
Face / Filler
Year-round

맨드라미 Coxcomb

Celosia cristata

Green and pale pink
Filler
Summer / Fall

장미 Rose
Rosa
'Amnesia'
Filler
Year-round

촛불 맨드라미 Celosia

Celosia spicata

Pink-purple
Gesture / Texture
Summer / Fall

아킬레아 Yarrow
Achillea millefolium

Pink-purple
Filler / Texture
Year-round

라일락 Lilac
Syringa vulgaris

'Beauty of Moscow'
Filler
Spring

투베로사 Tuberose
Polianthes tuberosa

'Pink Sapphire'
Gesture
Year-round

겹벚꽃 Cherry blossom
Prunus glandulosa

'Sinensis' double pink
Gesture / Filler
Spring

델피니움 Larkspur
Consolida regalis

Pale pink
Filler / Texture
Year-round

스위트피 Sweet pea
Lathyrus odoratus

Lavender
Texture / Filler / Gesture
Winter / Spring

캄파눌라 Campanula / bellflower
Campanula medium

Pale blue
Filler
Spring / Summer

스카비오사 Scabiosa

Scabiosa caucasica

Pale blue
Gesture
Year-round

스타티스 Statice

Limonium sinuatum

Pale blue
Filler
Year-round

아가판서스 Agapanthus
Agapanthus praecox

Blue
Texture / Filler
Year-round

니겔라 Nigella

Nigella damascena

Blue
Texture
Spring / Summer

암소니아 Blue Star
Amsonia tabernaemontana

Blue
Texture / Filler
Summer

알리움 Allium
Allium cepa
'Snake Ball'
Gesture
Spring

프리틸라리아 Fritilaria

Fritillaria hermonis

Green and brown
Gesture
Spring

맨드라미 Coxcomb

Celosia cristata

Pale green
Filler
Summer / Fall

프리틸라리아 Fritillaria
Fritillaria pontica

Green and brown
Gesture
Spring

헬레보러스 Hellebore

Helleborus x hybridus

Double green and purple
Face / Filler
Winter / Spring

프리틸라리아 Fritillaria
Fritillaria persica
'Ivory Bells'
Face / Gesture
Spring

헬레보러스 Hellebore

Helleborus x hybridus

Green and cream
Face / Filler
Winter / Spring

투베로사 Tuberose

Polianthes tuberosa

'The Pearl'
Gesture
Year-round

튤립 Tulip
Tulipa
'White Parrot'
Gesture
Spring

불두화 Vibernum

Viburnum opulus

'Roseum'
Filler
Spring

라넌큘러스 Ranunculus
Ranunculus asiaticus

Double green
Face / Filler
Winter / Spring

프렌치 패롯 튤립 French parrot tulip

Tulipa

Green
Gesture
Spring

헬레보러스 Hellebore

Helleborus x hybridus

Green and purple
Face / Filler
Winter / Spring

알리움 Allium / Sicilian onion
Allium siculum

Cream and brown
Texture
Spring

피어리스 Andromeda

Pieris japonica

White
Texture / Filler
Winter / Spring

퀸앤스레이스 Queen Anne's lace

Daucus carota

'Dara'
Gesture / Texture
Summer / Fall

헬레보러스 Hellebore / Christmas rose
Helleborus niger

Brown
Face / Filler
Winter / Spring

수국 Hydrangea

Hydrangea macrophylla

Brown and pink
Filler
Year-round

에레무르스 Foxtail Lily
Eremurus robustus

Peach
Gesture
Spring / Summer

장미 Rose
Rosa
'Koko Loko'
Face / Filler
Spring / Fall

왁스 플라워 Wax flower

Chamelaucium uncinatum

Pink and white variegated
Texture / Filler
Year-round

캥거루발톱 Kangaroo paw
Anigozanthos

Pink and orange
Texture
Year-round

라넌큘러스 Ranunculus
Ranunculus asiaticus
Double white and brown
Face / Filler
Winter / Spring

프리틸라리아 Snake's head fritillary

Fritillaria meleagris

Purple
Gesture / Texture
Spring

그레빌레아 Grevillea

Grevillea pteridifolia

Pale yellow
Gesture / Texture
Year-round

장미 Rose
Rosa
'Golden Mustard'
Filler
Year-round

스카비오사 Scabiosa

Scabiosa atropurpurea

Pale cream
Gesture
Year-round

캐모마일 Chamomile
Matricaria chamomilla

White and yellow
Texture / Filler
Year-round

수선화 Narcissus
Narcissus

'Bridal Crown'
Filler
Winter / Spring

부활절 백합 Easter lily
Lilium longiflorum

White
Face
Year-round

작약 Peony
Paeonia lactiflora
'Day Star'
Face
Spring

소국 Daisy mum
Chrysanthemum

Hybrid yellow
Filler
Year-round

파피오페딜럼 Lady's slipper orchid

Paphiopedilum

Yellow
Face
Year-round

장미 Rose
Rosa

Crocus Rose 'Ausquest'
Face / Filler
Spring / Fall

작약 Peony
Paeonia lactiflora
'Claire de Lune'
Face
Spring

작약 Peony
Paeonia lactiflora
'Lemon Dream'
Face
Spring

수선화 Narcissus
Narcissus
'Tahiti'
Gesture / Filler
Spring

글로리오사 Gloriosa lily

Gloriosa superba

'Lutea'
Texture / Gesture
Year-round

개나리 Forsythia

Forsythia x intermedia

Yellow
Gesture / Texture
Spring

팬지 Pansy

Viola hybrid

Yellow
Filler
Winter / Spring

튤립 Tulip
Tulipa
'Yellow Flight'
Gesture
Spring

프리지아 Freesia

Freesia

Double yellow
Filler
Year-round

튤립 Tulip
Tulipa

'Monte Spider'
Gesture
Spring

거베라 Gerbera daisy
Gerbera x hybrida
Butter yellow
Face
Year-round

버터플라이 라넌큘러스 Butterfly ranunculus
Ranunculus asiaticus

Yellow
Gesture / Filler
Winter / Spring

프렌치 패롯 튤립 French parrot tulip
Tulipa

Yellow
Gesture
Spring

풍년화 Witch hazel
Hamamelis x *intermedia*
Yellow
Gesture / Texture
Winter / Spring

온시디움 Oncidium orchid
Oncidium

Hybrid yellow
Filler / Gesture
Year-round

솔리다고 Goldenrod
Solidago canadensis

Yellow
Filler / Texture
Summer / Fall

미모사 Mimosa
Acacia retinodes

Yellow
Filler / Texture
Winter / Spring

수선화 Narcissus

Narcissus

'Soleil d'Or'
Filler
Winter / Spring

수선화 Daffodil

Narcissus pseudonarcissus

Yellow
Face
Winter / Spring

아킬레아 Yarrow
Achillea filipendulina
Gold
Filler / Texture
Year-round

금잔화 Calendula
Calendula officinalis

Yellow
Filler
Spring / Summer

라넌큘러스 Ranunculus
Ranunculus asiaticus

Clooney series, double yellow
Face / Filler
Winter / Spring

해바라기 Sunflower

Helianthus annuus

Yellow
Face
Summer

매리골드 French marigold
Tagetes patula

Striped mix
Texture / Gesture
Summer

프렌치 튤립 French tulip

Tulipa

Yellow and red
Gesture
Spring

온시디움 Oncidium orchid
Oncidium
Yellow
Gesture / Texture
Year-round

맨드라미 Coxcomb

Celosia cristata

Yellow
Filler
Summer / Fall

스위트피 Sweet pea
Lathyrus odoratus
Yellow dyed
Texture / Filler / Gesture
Winter / Spring

파피오페딜럼 Lady's slipper orchid
Paphiopedilum hybrid
Brown and green
Face
Year-round

백합 Lily
Lilium
'Solange'
Face
Year-round

장미 Rose
Rosa
'Combo'
Filler
Year-round

버터플라이 라넌큘러스 Butterfly ranunculus
Ranunculus asiaticus

Single orange
Gesture / Filler
Winter / Spring

산더소니아 Golden lantern lily
Sandersonia aurantiaca

Orange
Gesture / Texture
Spring / Summer

금잔화 Calendula
Calendula officinalis
'Indian Prince'
Filler
Spring / Summer

달리아 Dahlia
Dahlia

'Lakeview Lucky'
Face / Filler
Summer / Fall

아스클레피아스 Butterfly weed

Asclepias tuberosa

Orange
Filler / Texture
Year-round

글로리오사 Gloriosa lily

Gloriosa superba

Orange
Gesture
Year-round

수선화 Narcissus
Narcissus

'Johann Strauss'
Filler
Spring

극락조 Birds of Paradise
Strelitzia reginae

Orange
Face / Gesture
Year-round

라넌큘러스 Ranunculus
Ranunculus asiaticus
Gold and red variegated
Face / Filler
Winter / Spring

핀쿠션 프로테아 Pincushion protea

Leucospermum

'Carnival Orange'
Face / Texture
Year-round

에피덴드룸 Epidendrum

Epidendrum hybrid

Orange
Face / Gesture
Year-round

라넌큘러스 Ranunculus

Ranunculus asiaticus

Double orange
Face / Filler
Winter / Spring

오니소갈럼 Orange chincherinchee

Ornithogalum dubium

Orange
Filler
Year-round

프리틸라리아 Fritillaria
Fritillaria imperialis

Orange
Face / Gesture
Spring

아이슬란드 양귀비 Icelandic poppy

Papaver nudicaule

Peach
Face / Gesture
Winter / Spring

장미 Rose

Rosa

Renaissance series 'Claire'
Face / Filler
Spring / Fall

라넌큘러스 Ranunculus
Ranunculus asiaticus

Clooney series, peach
Face / Filler
Winter / Spring

천일홍 Gomphrena

Gomphrena globosa

Orange
Filler
Summer / Fall

안수리움 Anthurium
Anthurium

'Rothschildianum'
Face
Year-round

칼라 Calla lily
Zantedeschia

'Mango'
Gesture / Filler
Year-round

말나리 계 Martagon hybrid
Lilium x martagon
'Orange Marmalade'
Gesture / Texture
Summer

프렌치 튤립 French tulip
Tulipa
'Flaming Parrot'
Gesture
Spring

달리아 Dahlia

Dahlia

'Iced Tea'
Face / Filler
Summer / Fall

아이슬란드 양귀비 Icelandic poppy

Papaver nudicaule

Orange
Gesture / Face
Winter / Spring

헬리코니아 Heliconia
Heliconia stricta
Red
Face
Year-round

맨드라미 Plumosa celosia

Celosia argentea

Rust
Filler / Texture
Summer / Fall

튤립 Tulip
Tulipa
'Leo'
Gesture
Spring

국화 Spider mum

Chrysanthemum

Orange and yellow
Face / Filler
Fall

장미 Rose
Rosa
'Toffee'
Filler
Year-round

안수리움 Anthurium

Anthurium

'Hawaii'
Face
Year-round

맨드라미 Coxcomb

Celosia cristata

Rust
Filler
Summer / Fall

국화 Spider mum
Chrysanthemum

'Seaton's Toffee'
Face / Filler
Fall

온시디움 Oncidium orchid
Oncidium hybrid

Orange and brown
Gesture / Texture
Year-round

제임스 스토리 James Story orchid
Oncidium hybrid
Yellow and brown
Gesture / Texture
Year-round

아마릴리스 Amaryllis
Hippeastrum cybister
'Tarantula'
Face
Winter

사라세니아 Pitcher plant
Sarracenia leucophylla
Red and white variegated
Texture
Spring / Summer

스위트피 Sweet pea
Lathyrus odoratus

Brown dyed
Texture / Filler / Gesture
Winter / Spring

라넌큘러스 Ranunculus

Ranunculus asiaticus

'Charlotte' peach
Face
Winter / Spring

독일붓꽃 Beared iris
Iris germanica
Purple and brown
Face
Spring

달리아 Dahlia
Dahlia

'Bahama Apricot'
Face
Summer / Fall

달리아 Dahlia
Dahlia
'Cornel Bronze'
Face / Filler
Summer / Fall

달리아 Dahlia
Dahlia
'Gitts Crazy'
Face
Summer / Fall

안수리움 Anthurium
Anthurium

'Cognac'
Face
Year-round

모란 Tree Peony
Paeonia x suffruticosa
'Callie's Memory'
Face
Spring

장미 Rose
Rosa
'Kahala'
Filler
Year-round

아마릴리스 Amaryllis

Hippeastrum

'Rilona'
Face
Winter

산당화 Quince
Chaenomeles speciosa
Red
Gesture
Winter / Spring

백일홍 Zinnia

Zinnia elegans

Coral
Face / Filler
Summer

산당화 Quince

Chaenomeles japonica

Coral
Gesture
Winter / Spring

아이슬란드 양귀비 Icelandic poppy

Papaver nudicaule

Watermelon
Face / Gesture
Winter / Spring

달리아 Dahlia
Dahlia

'Amber Queen'
Face / Filler
Summer / Fall

크리스마스 부쉬 Christmas Bush

Ceratopetalum gummiferum

'Albery's Red'
Texture / Filler
Fall / Winter

달리아 Dahlia

Dahlia

Pale red
Face / Filler
Summer / Fall

카네이션 Carnation

Dianthus

Pink and red
Filler
Year-round

코스모스 Cosmos

Cosmos atrosanguineus
Dark red
Gesture
Summer / Fall

버터플라이 라넌큘러스 Butterfly ranunculus
Ranunculus asiaticus

Double rust
Gesture / Filler
Winter / Spring

달리아 Dahlia

Dahlia

'Red and White Fubuki'
Face
Summer / Fall

프렌치 튤립 French tulip
Tulipa
'Kingsblood'
Gesture
Spring

헬리코니아 Heliconia
Heliconia vellerigera
'King Kong'
Face
Year-round

아마릴리스 Amaryllis

Hippeastrum

'Simply Red'
Face
Winter

틸란시아 Quill
Tillandsia cyanea hybrid
Red
Filler
Year-round

거베라 Gerbera daisy
Gerbera x *hybrida*
Red
Face
Year-round

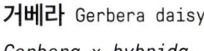

안수리움 Anthurium

Anthurium andraeanum

Red
Face
Year-round

시클라멘 Cyclamen
Cyclamen persicum
Red
Filler
Spring

프렌치 패롯 튤립 French parrot tulip

Tulipa

'Red Parrot'
Gesture
Spring

스프레이 카네이션 Spray carnation
Dianthus

'Solomio Amos'
Texture / Filler
Year-round

백일홍 Zinnia

Zinnia elegans

Double red
Face / Filler
Summer

아네모네 Anemone

Anemone coronaria

Red
Face
Winter / Spring

라넌큘러스 Ranunculus
Ranunculus asiaticus

Dark red
Face / Filler
Winter / Spring

맨드라미 Coxcomb
Celosia cristata

Dark red
Filler
Summer / Fall

장미 Rose
Rosa
'Red Piano'
Face / Filler
Year-round

달리아 Dahlia

Dahlia

Dark red
Face
Summer / Fall

장미 Rose
Rosa
Black Magic 'Tankalcig'
Filler
Year-round

튤립 Tulip

Tulipa

'Black Hero'
Gesture
Spring

라넌큘러스 Ranunculus

Ranunculus asiaticus

Red and brown variegated
Face / Filler
Winter / Spring

작약 Peony
Paeonia lactiflora
'Black Swan'
Face
Spring

작약 Peony

Paeonia lactiflora

'Chocolate Soldier'
Face
Spring

종이꽃 Straw flower

Xerochrysum bracteatum

Burgundy
Filler / Texture
Summer / Fall

아스틸베 Astilbe
Astilbe
'Red Sentinel'
Texture
Year-round

수국 Hydrangea

Hydrangea macrophylla
Dark pink
Filler
Year-round

심비디움 Cymbidium orchid
Cymbidium hybrid

Dark pink
Face / Gesture
Year-round

리시안셔스 Lisianthus
Eustoma russellianum

Brown and purple variegated
Filler
Year-round

모란 Tree peony

Paeonia x suffruticosa

Dark pink and peach
Face
Spring

라넌큘러스 Ranunculus
Ranunculus asiaticus
Dark pink
Face / Filler
Winter / Spring

아네모네 Anenome

Anemone coronaria

Red and white variegated
Face
Winter / Spring

달리아 Dahlia
Dahlia

'Sonic Bloom'
Face
Summer / Fall

알피니아 Ginger

Alpinia purpurata

Red
Face
Year-round

스위트피 Sweet pea
Lathyrus odoratus

Red
Texture / Filler / Gesture
Winter / Spring

진달래 Azalea
Rhododendron molle
Pink hybrid
Filler
Spring

장미 Rose
Rosa
'Pink Piano'
Face / Filler
Year-round

장미 Rose
Rosa
Kate 'Auschris'
Face / Filler
Spring / Fall

장미 Rose
Rosa
'Pink Floyd'
Filler
Year-round

스위트피 Sweet pea
Lathyrus odoratus

Coral
Texture / Filler / Gesture
Winter / Spring

라넌큘러스 Ranunculus
Ranunculus asiaticus
Double pink and green
Face / Filler
Winter / Spring

작약 Peony
Paeonia

'Coral Charm'
Face
Spring

300

장미 Rose
Rosa
Benjamin Britten 'Ausencart'
Face / Filler
Spring / Fall

와라타 Waratah

Telopea speciosissima

Pink
Face / Texture
Summer / Fall

장미 Rose
Rosa
'Romantic Antike'
Face / Filler
Year-round

안수리움 Anthurium
Anthurium

'Marea'
Face
Year-round

작약 Peony

Paeonia lactiflora

'Dr Alexander Fleming'
Face
Spring

장미 Rose
Rosa
'Lady Moon'
Filler
Year-round

라넌큘러스 Ranunculus
Ranunculus asiaticus
Double pink
Face / Filler
Winter / Spring

프렌치 튤립 French tulip

Tulipa

Pink
Gesture
Spring

리시안셔스 Lisianthus

Eustoma russellianum

Double pink
Filler
Year-round

스타티스 Statice

Limonium sinuatum

Pink
Filler
Year-round

금낭화 Bleeding heart
Lamprocapnos spectabilis
Pink
Gesture / Texture
Spring

달리아 Dahlia
Dahlia

'Lagoon'
Face
Summer / Fall

작약 Peony

Paeonia lactiflora

'Nymphe'
Face
Spring

라넌큘러스 Ranunculus

Ranunculus asiaticus
'Charlotte' burgundy and white
Face
Winter / Spring

수련 Water lily

Nymphaea

Pink
Face
Year-round

에키네시아 Echinacea
Echinacea purpurea
Pink
Face / Filler
Summer

스카비오사 Scabiosa

Scabiosa columbaria

Pink
Gesture
Year-round

작약 Peony

Paeonia lactiflora

'Sarah Bernhardt'
Face
Spring

라넌큘러스 Ranunculus
Ranunculus asiaticus

Clooney series, pale pink
Face / Filler
Winter / Spring

매화나무 Plum blossom
Prunus mume

Pink
Gesture
Spring

목련 Magnolia
Magnolia x *soulangeana*
'Alexandrina'
Face / Gesture
Spring

장미 Rose

Rosa

'Royal Amethyst'
Face / Filler
Spring / Fall

아네모네 Anemone
Anemone coronaria

Double magenta
Face
Winter / Spring

불로초 Sedum

Hylotelephium telephium
Pink
Filler
Summer / Fall

추명국 Autumn anemone / Japanese anemone
Anemone hupehensis

Pale purple
Gesture
Fall

거베라 Gerbera Daisy
Gerbera x hybrida
Double dark pink
Face
Year-round

헬레보러스 Hellebore

Helleborus x *hybridus*

Dark pink
Face / Filler
Winter

백일홍 Zinnia
Zinnia elegans
'Queen Lime Blush'
Filler
Summer

그레빌레아 Grevillea

Grevillea

'Robyn Gordon'
Gesture / Texture
Year-round

디기탈리스 Foxglove
Digitalis purpurea

Purple
Gesture / Face
Spring / Summer

스위트피 Sweet pea
Lathyrus odoratus
Purple and white variegated
Texture / Filler / Gesture
Winter / Spring

헤더 Heather
Calluna vulgaris
Dark pink
Texture / Filler
Year-round

달리아 Dahlia

Dahlia

'Koko Puff'
Face / Filler
Summer / Fall

보로니아 Boronia
Boronia heterophylla
Purple
Filler / Texture
Spring

시레네 Sweet William catchfly
Silene armeria
Purple
Texture / Filler
Spring

안수리움 Anthurium
Anthurium

'Previa'
Face
Year-round

달리아 Dahlia
Dahlia

'Mikayla Miranda'
Face
Summer / Fall

국화 Chrysanthemum

Chrysanthemum

Lilac
Filler
Year-round

장미 Rose
Rosa
'Menta'
Filler
Year-round

스위트피 Sweet pea
Lathyrus odoratus
'Matucana'
Texture / Filler / Gesture
Winter / Spring

패롯 튤립 Parrot tulip
Tulipa
'Blue Parrot'
Gesture
Spring

341

델피니움 Delphinium
Delphinium

Lavender
Gesture / Face
Year-round

리아트리스 Liatris
Liatris spicata

Purple
Gesture
Year-round

라넌큘러스 Ranunculus
Ranunculus asiaticus

Purple and mauve variegated
Face / Filler
Winter / Spring

아스트란시아 Astrantia

Astrantia major

'Rosensinfonie'
Texture / Filler
Year-round

독일붓꽃 Bearded iris

Iris germanica

'Indian Chief'
Face
Spring

스위트피 Sweet pea
Lathyrus odoratus
Chocolate dyed
Texture / Filler / Gesture
Winter / Spring

리시안셔스 Lisianthus

Eustoma russellianum

Dark purple
Filler
Year-round

헬레보러스 Hellebore

Helleborus x hybridus

Dark purple
Face / Filler
Winter / Spring

알리움 Allium
Allium cepa
Purple and gray
Gesture
Spring

라일락 Lilac
Syringa

Lavender
Texture / Filler
Spring

온시디움 Oncidium orchid
Oncidium hybrid

'Kauai'
Gesture
Year-round

스위트피 Sweet pea

Lathyrus odoratus

'Chocolate Flake'
Texture / Filler / Gesture
Winter / Spring

루피너스 Lupine

Lupinus x regalis

Blue
Gesture
Spring / Summer

클레마티스 Clematis
Clematis alpina

'Tage Lundell' lavender
Gesture / Filler
Year-round

헬레보러스 Hellebore

Helleborus x hybridus

Double pink and white variegated
Face / Filler
Winter / Spring

벨 클레마티스 Bell clematis

Clematis

'Rooguchi' purple
Gesture
Spring

캥거루발톱 Kangaroo paw
Anigozanthos flavidus
'Ember' purple variegated
Gesture / Texture
Year-round

스위트피 Sweet pea

Lathyrus nervosus

Purple
Texture / Filler / Gesture
Winter / Spring

벨 클레마티스 Bell clematis

Clematis

'Rooguchi' blue
Gesture
Spring

시네라리아 Cineraria

Pericallis x *hybrida*

Blue
Texture / Filler
Spring

수련 Water lily

Nymphaea nouchali

Lavender
Face
Year-round

아네모네 Anemone

Anemone coronaria

Lavender
Face
Winter / Spring

아게라텀 Floss flower

Ageratum houstonianum

Purple
Filler
Summer

클레마티스 Clematis

Clematis lanuginosa

Purple
Face
Year-round

베로니카 Veronica

Veronica longifolia

Purple
Gesture
Year-round

과꽃 China aster
Callistephus chinensis
Double blue
Filler
Summer

라벤더 Lavender
Lavandula x *intermedia*
Lavender
Gesture / Texture
Year-round

수국 Hydrangea
Hydrangea macrophylla
Pale purple variegated
Filler
Year-round

히아신스 Hyacinth
Hyacinthus orientalis
'Delft Blue'
Filler
Spring

물망초 Forget-me-not
Myosotis sylvatica

Blue
Gesture
Winter / Spring

델피니움 Larkspur
Consolida regalis
Pale blue
Gesture / Texture
Year-round

무스카리 Muscari

Muscari botryoides

Blue
Gesture / Texture
Winter / Spring

알리움 Allium

Allium caeruleum

Blue
Gesture
Spring

옥시페탈룸 Tweedia

Tweedia caerulea

Blue
Filler
Year-round

수레국화 Cornflower
Centaurea cyanus

Blue
Gesture / Filler
Spring

아이리스 Iris

Iris latifolia

Blue
Gesture / Filler
Spring

에린기움 Blue thistle

Eryngium planum

Blue
Texture
Year-round

델피니움 Delphinium

Delphinium

Blue
Gesture / Face
Year-round

수국 Hydrangea
Hydrangea macrophylla
Blue
Filler
Year-round

미니 델피니움 Larkspur

Consolida regalis

Dark blue
Gesture / Texture
Year-round

서양매발톱꽃 Columbine
Aquilegia vulgaris var.stellata
'Black Barlow'
Gesture / Texture
Summer

독일붓꽃 Bearded iris
Iris germanica
'Black Knight'
Face
Spring

스카비오사 Scabiosa

Scabiosa atropurpurea
Dark red
Gesture
Year-round

모란 Tree peony

Paeonia x suffruticosa

'Vesuvian'
Face
Spring

거베라 Gerbera daisy
Gerbera x hybrida
Dark red
Face / Filler
Year-round

작약 Peony
Paeonia lactiflora
'Black Panther'
Face
Spring

스프레이 카네이션 Spray carnation
Dianthus

Pink and purple variegated
Texture / Filler
Year-round

파피오페딜럼 Lady's slipper orchid
Paphiopedilum
Burgundy
Face
Year-round

모란 Tree peony
Paeonia x suffruticosa
'Burgundy Wine'
Face
Spring

촛불 맨드라미 Plumosa celosia
Celosia argentea
Dark red
Texture / Filler
Summer / Fall

코스모스 Cosmos

Cosmos bipinnatus

'Rubenza'
Gesture
Summer

장미 Rose
Rosa
'Flash Night'
Filler
Year-round

패롯 튤립 Parrot tulip

Tulipa

'Rococo'
Gesture
Spring

말나리 계 Martagon hybrid
Lilium x dalhansonii
Dark red
Gesture / Texture
Year-round

백일홍 Zinnia
Zinnia elegans

Persian carpet mix
Texture / Filler
Summer / Fall

튤립 Tulip
Tulipa

Brown
Gesture
Spring

심비디움 Cymbidium orchid
Cymbidium hybrid
Brown
Face / Gesture
Year-round

프리틸라리아 Fritillaria
Fritillaria uva-vulpis

Brown and yellow
Gesture
Spring

사라세니아 Pitcher plant
Sarracenia x moorei
Dark burgundy
Texture
Summer

칼라 Calla lily

Zantedeschia

'Red Star'
Gesture / Filler
Year-round

카네이션 Carnation
Dianthus

Dark purple
Filler
Year-round

튤립 Tulip

Tulipa

'Black Jack'
Gesture
Spring

루드베키아 Black Eyed Susan
Rudbeckia hirta
'Cherry Brandy'
Face / Filler
Summer

해바라기 Sunflower

Helianthus annuus

'Black Beauty'
Face
Summer

프리틸라리아 Fritillaria

Fritillaria persica

Dark purple
Face / Gesture
Winter / Spring

달리아 Dahlia
Dahlia

'Kokucho'
Face
Fall

달리아 Dahlia
Dahlia
'Crossfield Ebony'
Face / Filler
Summer / Fall

달리아 Dahlia
Dahlia
'Karma Choc'
Face
Summer / Fall

라넌큘러스 Ranunculus
Ranunculus asiaticus
Black
Face / Filler
Winter / Spring

코스모스 Cosmos

Cosmos atrosanguineus

'Chocamocha'
Gesture
Summer / Fall

헬레보러스 Hellebore
Helleborus x hybridus
Double black
Face / Filler
Winter / Spring

안수리움 Anthurium

Anthurium

'Karma Black'
Face
Year-round

스카비오사 Scabiosa
Scabiosa atropurpurea
Black
Gesture
Year-round

칼라 Calla lily
Zantedeschia

'Black Star'
Gesture
Year-round

부록

Notes

꽃을 구매하기 전

어떤 행사를 위해 꽃을 구매하는지 알아야 한다. 예를 들어, 디너 파티를 위한 커다란 센터피스를 만들려고 하는가? 아니면 심플한 화병에 한 종류의 꽃을 담아 당신의 집에 두려고 하는가? 꽃을 구매하기 전 당신이 꼭 물어봐야 할 질문으로는 어떤 행사를 위한 꽃인가? 어디에 꽃을 둘 것인가? 등이 있다.

꽃시장은 집안 장식용 꽃을 구매할 수 있는 최고의 장소이다. 이곳의 꽃은 주로 지역 화훼 농장에서 직접 출하되어 판매된다.

Notes

기본적인 꽃 관리

결국, 꽃 관리의 모든 것은 수분관리에 달려있다. 수분 공급이 잘 된 꽃은 더 신선해 보이고 꽃의 수명도 더 길다.

꽃시장에서 귀가하는 즉시, 물에 담가야 하는 것은 모두 사선으로 다시 잘라주어야 한다.

항상 날이 날카로운 클리퍼를 사용하라. 무딘 클리퍼는 잘릴 때의 눌림으로 줄기가 짓이겨질 수 있다.

꽃의 재수화(conditioning, 물올림)를 위해 준비한 물통과, 꽃을 꽂기 위해 준비한 화병은 비누로 문질러 씻은 후 물로 헹궈준다. 자칫 물통이나 꽃병에 남아있는 미생물로 인하여 꽃이 빨리 시들 수 있기 때문이다.

절화 보존제(flower food: 당을 포함한 혼합물이며 구입하거나 직접 만들 수 있다)를 물에 첨가한다.

대부분의 꽃은 차가운 물을 사용해야 한다. 그러나 목련이나 장미처럼 단단한 줄기를 가진 꽃은 개화를 촉진시키기 위해 미온수나 실온의 물로 대체할 수 있다. 이 경우, 단기에 물올림이 되어 수분이 빠른 속도로 꽃까지 전달된다.

물 속으로 잠기는 잎들은 모두 자르거나 제거해야 한다. 그렇지 않으면 미생물이 쉽게 번식한다. 꽃에 잎이 적을수록 수분이 꽃으로 빨리 공급된다.

꽃은 항상 선선한 곳에 둔다. 열기는 꽃을 시들게 한다. 외풍을 피하라.

Notes

라일락처럼 목질화된 꽃은 물의 흡수를 최대화하기 위해 줄기 하단의 외피를 벗겨내고 줄기 위쪽을 향해 세로로 여러 차례 가늘게 쪼갠다.

양귀비는 물에 넣기 전 탄화처리(cauterized)가 필요하다. 양귀비의 줄기 끝을 자르고 그 절단면을 라이터나 불을 이용하여 줄기 끝에서 2~5cm 정도를 살짝 태워 찬물에 넣는다.

수국은 꽃잎으로도 수분을 흡수하기 때문에 충분한 수분 공급을 위해서는 줄기를 물에 담그는 것 뿐 아니라 꽃잎에도 물을 분무해 주는 것이 좋다. 사실, 물을 분무해 주는 것은 대부분의 꽃에 이롭다. 특별히 날씨가 덥거나, 여건상 미리 꽃꽂이를 해 두어야 하는 상황이거나 행사가 있는 경우, 물을 분무해 주면 꽃이 싱싱하게 유지될 수 있다.

Notes

필수 도구

클리퍼 Clippers

- 절화 또는 부드러운 잎 등의 절지를 할 때 사용한다. 무딘 클리퍼는 줄기를 자를 때의 눌림으로 도관이 막힐 수 있으니 이를 방지하기 위해 날을 날카롭게 관리해 두는 것이 좋다.

정원용 큰 가위 Garden shears

- 두꺼운 나뭇가지나 목질화된 줄기를 자를 때 사용한다.

절화용 칼 Floral knife

- 줄기의 표면 또는 나무껍질을 벗겨낼 때 그리고 줄기를 자를 때 사용한다.

투명 플로럴 테이프 Clear floral tape

- 일반 투명 접착테이프보다 내구성이 강하다. 철망을 사용할 수 없는 유리병이나 투명 화병의 입구에 격자모양의 테이프 그리드(Tape grids)를 만들 때 사용한다.

코팅된 그린 플로럴 철사 Green-coated floral wire: 마법의 도구!

- 화훼 구조물, 화환, 화관 등을 만들 때 사용한다. 꽃을 단단하게 묶거나 고정시킬 때 사용하는 다재다능한 도구이다. 코팅된 그린 플로럴 철사는 여러 가지 두께로 유통된다.

철사 절단기 Wire clippers

- 철사를 자를 때 절화용 클리퍼를 사용해서는 안 된다. 클리퍼가 금세 무디어진다.

Notes

침봉 Floral pin, kenzan

- 유리로 만든 그릇 등 얕은 화기에 절화나 절지를 고정하는 도구로 사용한다. 이케바나를 할 때 주로 사용한다.

오아시스 픽스 Floral putty

- 오아시스 픽스는 접착력이 있는 점토로서 플로럴 프로그(Floral frog: 꽃을 고정시키는 구조물)를 포함한 다른 소재들이 움직이지 않도록 고정하기 위해 사용한다. 오아시스 픽스는 다양한 표면에 적용이 가능하다.

코팅된 철망 Coated chicken wire

- 화훼 장식과 구조물의 형태를 만들거나 기본 토대를 만들 때 사용한다.

그린 플로럴 스틱 Green floral sticks

- 과일에 그린 플로럴 스틱을 찔러 사용하면 화훼 장식에 과일을 더할 수 있다. 화훼 조형물을 만들 때 플로럴 스틱과 워터튜브를 연결하면 짧은 줄기를 길게 사용할 수 있다.

그린 플로럴 테이프 Green floral tape

- 높은 접착력이 필요할 때 사용하는 강력한 플로럴 테이프이다.
- 워터 튜브(Water picks)를 플로럴 스틱에 붙일 때 사용한다
- 유리가 아닌 재질의 화기에 접착할 때 사용한다. 특히 금속이나 돌로 만들어진 용기 안에 치킨 와이어를 고정할 때 사용한다.

워터 튜브 Water pick

- 물을 필요로 하는 꽃의 길이를 연장하고자 할 때 필요하다. 물을 채운 워터튜브에 줄기를 넣고 그린 플로럴 스틱에 테이프를 감아 사용한다.

Notes

화병 준비하기

피쳐, 위로 긴 화병
- 한 종류의 꽃 또는 절지를 사용한 다발을 담기에 좋다.
- 특별한 사전 준비를 할 필요는 없다. 사용 전 세척만 하면 된다.

원통형, 나팔 모양의 화병
- DIY 꽃꽂이를 위한 좋은 선택이다.
- 투명 플로럴 테이프를 사용하여 화병 입구에 간단한 격자무늬의 테이프 그리드를 만든다. 그러면 꽃이 움직이지 않고 그 위치에 고정된다.
- 정교한 작업을 위해서는 플로럴 프로그를 사용하고, 화병 입구에는 조금 더 촘촘한 격자 무늬의 테이프 그리드를 만든 후 꽃꽂이를 하는 것이 좋다.
- 격자가 많을수록 더 정교한 꽃을 만들 수 있다.

유리 보울, 콤포트
- 플로럴 프로그를 오아시스 픽스를 이용해 용기 바닥에 접착한다. 아주 견고한 구조가 필요할 때는 투명 테이프로 격자 무늬를 만들어 병용하도록 한다.

다리가 있는 그릇, 단지, 콤포트
- 일반적으로 센터피스를 만들 때 사용하는 용기이다. 그릇의 다리로 인하여 전반적인 높이가 높아지기 때문에 용기 밖으로 풍성하게 늘어지는 화훼 장식을 할 수 있어 생동감 있는 꽃꽂이가 가능하다.
- 불투명한 화병일 경우, 철망을 사용해서 구조를 만든다
  - 철망을 용기 입구의 3과 1/2 크기의 사각형 모양으로 자른다.
  - 사각의 네 면을 연결해 박스 형태를 만들고 각 모서리를 접어 공모양으로 만든다.
  - 구 형태의 철망을 화병에 맞추어 넣는다.

Notes

· 플로럴 테이프를 사용하여 철망 위를 'X'모양으로 붙여 철망이 원하는 위치에서 움직이지 않도록 고정한다.
· 꽃을 꽂을 때, 줄기가 구 형태로 말린 철망의 두개 층을 통과하여 안정적으로 고정되었는지 확인하도록 한다.

Notes

추천 컬러 팔레트

- White, cream, green and blush 흰색, 크림색, 녹색 및 엷은 분홍색
- Chartreuse, light yellow, cream and white 연두색, 연노란색, 크림색 및 흰색
- Peach, light yellow, cream and brown 복숭아색, 연노란색, 크림색 및 갈색
- Yellow, lavender and white 노란색, 연보라색 및 흰색
- Orange, peach and gold with pop of blue 주황색, 복숭아색, 금색 그리고 약간의 파란색
- Rust, coral, red and cream 적갈색, 산호색, 적색 및 크림색
- Pink, brown and white 분홍색, 갈색 및 흰색
- Blue, yellow and cream 파란색, 노란색 및 크림색
- Lavender, chartreuse and dark green 연보라색, 연두색 및 어두운 녹색
- Mauve, blush and dark burgundy 담자색, 엷은 분홍색 및 진홍색
- Burgundy, deep green and fuchsia 진홍색, 짙은 녹색 및 자홍색
- Purple, cream and black 보라색, 크림색 및 검정색

Notes

환경을 고려한 지속 가능성에 관하여

우리는 세계 어디로든 꽃을 운반할 수 있는 글로벌한 시대에 살고 있다. 그리고 우리는 화훼 산업이 때때로 엄청난 폐기물을 야기할 수 있다는 사실을 깨달았다. 특히 대규모 행사 직후 버려지는 꽃들은 막대한 폐기물의 발생 원인이 된다. 하지만 전문 행사 기획자들과 플로리스트들이 환경보호를 위해 실천의 작은 한 걸음을 내딛는다면 환경을 고려한 지속가능한 발전에 큰 도움이 될 것이라고 생각한다.

- 가능한 한 제철의 꽃을 사용하고, 지역에서 재배된 꽃을 구매한다.

- 행사 후 발생하는 모든 유기물은 퇴비로 만들고, 이 비용은 예산에 포함시키도록 한다.

- 가진 것을 나눈다. 어떤 도시에서는 행사 후 사용된 꽃을 수거해서 병원이나 기타 다른 기관으로 재분배하는 서비스를 시행하고 있다.

- 환경을 오염시킬 수 있는 플로럴 폼 Floral foam과 같은 일회용품은 피하도록 한다. 플로럴 프로그, 철망 그리고 화병은 모두 재활용이 가능하다.

Notes

옥시페탈룸
Tweedia

Tweedia caerulea

'Pint White'
Filler
Year-round

수국
Hydrangea

Hydrangea macrophylla

White
Filler
Year-round

시클라멘
Cyclamen

Cyclamen persicum

White
Filler
Spring

진달래
Azalea

Rhododendron molle

White
Filler
Spring

라넌큘러스
Ranunculus

Ranunculus asiaticus

Double white
Face / Filler
Winter / Spring

스톡
Stock

Matthiola incana

Double white
Gesture / Filler
Year-round

캥거루 발톱
Kangaroo paw

Anigozanthos

'Bush Diamond'
Gesture / Texture
Year-round

벚나무
Flowering cherry

Prunus × subhirtella

'Autumnalis' white
Gesture / Filler
Spring

장미
Rose

Rosa

'Tibet'
Filler
Year-round

수선화
Paper white

Narcissus papyraceus

White
Filler
Winter / spring

델피니움
Delphinium

Delphinium

'Centurion White'
Face / Gesture
Year-round

플란넬 플라워
Flannel flower

Actinotus helianthi

White
Filler / Texture
Winter / Spring

스카비오사
Scabiosa

Scabiosa columbaria

White
Gesture
Year-round

스프레이 카네이션
Spray carnation

Dianthus

'Grenadin White'
Texture / Filler
Year-round

백합
Lily

Lilium

'Premium Blond'
Face
Year-round

코와니
Allium / Naples onion

Allium neapolitanum

White
Gesture / Texture
Spring / Summer

아네모네
Anemone

Anemone

De Caen Group white
Face
Winter / Spring

조팝나무
Spirea

Spiraea

'Arguta'
Gesture / Texture
Winter / Spring

아네모네
Anemone

Anemone coronaria

Single white
Face
Winter / Spring

네리네
Nerine

Nerine bowdenii

'Pallida' white
Filler / Texture
Year-round

작약
Peony
Paeonia
'Bowl of Cream'
Face
Spring

스프레이 카네이션
Spray carnation
Dianthus
'Star Snow Tessino'
Filler / Texture
Year-round

장미
Rose
Rosa
'White Majolica'
Filler
Year-round

장미
Rose
Rosa
Winchester Cathedral 'Auscat'
Face / Filler
Spring / Fall

라일락
Lilac
Syringa vulgaris
White
Filler
Spring

아스트란시아
Astrantia
Astrantia major
'White Giant'
Texture / Filler
Year-round

칼라
Calla lily
Zantedeschia aethiopica
White
Face / Gesture
Year-round

아마릴리스
Amaryllis
Hippeastrum
'White Dazzler'
Face
Winter

프리지아
Freesia
Freesia
White
Filler
Year-round

글라디올러스
Gladiolus
Gladiolus
'White Prosperity'
Gesture
Year-round

글라디올러스
Gladiolus
Gladiolus × colvillii
'Albus'
Gesture
Summer / Fall

달리아
Dahlia
Dahlia
'Blizzard'
Face
Summer / Fall

장미
Rose
Rosa
'Garden Snow'
Filler
Year-round

히아신스
Hyacinth
Hyacinthus orientalis
White
Filler
Winter / Spring

튤립
Tulip
Tulipa
'White Liberstar'
Gesture
Spring

수선화
Narcissus
Narcissus poeticus hybrid
White
Face / Filler
Winter / Spring

리시마치아
Gooseneck loosestrife
Lysimachia clethroides
White
Gesture
Summer

무스카리
Muscari
Muscari azureum
'Album'
Texture / Filler
Winter / Spring

둥글레
Solomon's seal
Polygonatum biflorum
White
Gesture
Spring

은방울꽃
Lily of the valley
Convallaria majalis
White
Texture
Spring

스노플레이크 Snowflake *Leucojum aestivum* White Texture Winter	**스위트피** Sweet pea *Lathyrus odoratus* White Texture / Filler / Gesture Winter / Spring	**거베라** Gerbera daisy *Gerbera x hybrida* White Face / Gesture Year-round	**리시안셔스** Lisianthus *Eustoma russellianum* White Filler Year-round
튤립 Tulip *Tulipa* 'Honeymoon' Gesture Spring	**글라디올러스** Gladiolus *Gladiolus* 'The Bride' Gesture / Filler Summer	**아스틸베** Astilbe *Astilbe* 'Deutschland' Texture Year-round	**스위트피** Everlasting pea *Lathyrus latifolius* 'Albus' white Texture / Filler / Gesture Winter / Spring
코스모스 Cosmos *Cosmos bipinnatus* Double white Gesture Summer	**달리아** Dahlia *Dahlia* 'Figaro' White Face Summer / Fall	**안수리움** Anthurium *Anthurium* 'Acropolis' Face Year-round	**칼라** Calla lily *Zantedeschia* 'Aspen' Gesture Year-round
안수리움 Anthurium *Anthurium* 'Lumina' Face Year-round	**작약** Peony *Paeonia lactiflora* 'Festiva Maxima' Face Spring	**디디스쿠스** Blue lace flower *Trachymene coerulea* 'Lacy Pink' Gesture Spring / Summer	**니겔라** Nigella *Nigella damascena* White Texture Spring / Summer
조팝나무 Spirea *Spiraea thunbergii* White Gesture / Texture Winter / Spring	**라이스플라워** Heath rice flower *Pimelea phylicoides* White Texture Spring / Summer	**왁스 플라워** Wax flower *Chamelaucium uncinatum* White Texture / Filler Year-round	**산당화** Quince *Chaenomeles speciosa* 'Nivalis' white Gesture Winter

작약 Peony *Paeonia lactiflora* 'Duchesse de Nemours' Face Spring	**스위트피** Sweet pea *Lathyrus odoratus* Pale pink Texture / Filler / Gesture Winter / Spring	**작약** Peony *Paeonia lactiflora* 'Rooster Reveille' Face Spring	**작약** Peony *Paeonia lactiflora* 'Sonata' Face Spring
디기탈리스 Foxglove *Digitalis purpurea* f. albiflora Gesture / Face Spring / Summer	**산딸나무** Dogwood *Cornus kousa* var. chinensis Gesture / Filler Spring	**온시디움** Oncidium orchid *Oncidium hybrid* White and pink Texture / Gesture Year-round	**버터플라이 라넌큘러스** Butterfly ranunculus *Ranunculus asiaticus* 'Butterfly Lux' cream Gesture / Filler Winter / Spring
수선화 Narcissus *Narcissus* 'Salome' Face / Filler Spring	**재스민** Jasmine *Jasminum polyanthum* White and pink Texture Winter / Spring	**장미** Rose *Rosa* 'Charity' Filler Spring / Fall	**장미** Rose *Rosa* 'Champagne' Filler Year-round
히아신스 Hyacinth *Hyacinthus orientalis* Pale pink Filler Winter / Spring	**아스틸베** Astilbe *Astilbe* 'Elizabeth Bloom' Texture Year-round	**스톡** Stock *Matthiola incana* Double peach Filler / Gesture Year-round	**백합** Lily *Lilium* Pink roselily Face Year-round
장미 Rose *Rosa* 'Sahara' Filler Year-round	**에피덴드룸** Epidendrum *Epidendrum* hybrid Pale pink Gesture Year-round	**국화** Chrysanthemum *Chrysanthemum* 'Seaton's Je Dore' Face Fall	**달리아** Dahlia *Dahlia* 'Cream and Pink' Face Summer / Fall

팬지
Pansy
Viola hybrid
Pale pink and yellow
Filler
Winter / Spring

스타티스
Statice
Limonium sinuatum
Peach
Texture
Year-round

독일붓꽃
Bearded iris
Iris germanica
'Party Dress'
Face
Spring

튤립
Tulip
Tulipa
'Apricot Beauty'
Gesture
Spring

카네이션
Carnation
Dianthus
Nude
Filler
Year-round

장미
Rose
Rosa
'Sahara Sensation'
Filler
Year-round

스톡
Stock
Matthiola incana
Single petal peach
Gesture / Filler
Year-round

장미
Rose
Rosa
'Cappuccino'
Filler
Year-round

백합
Lily
Lilium
Peach
Face
Year-round

리시안셔스
Lisianthus
Eustoma russellianum
Peach
Filler
Year-round

장미
Rose
Rosa
Juliet 'Ausjameson'
Face / Filler
Year-round

달리아
Dahlia
Dahlia
'Cafe au Lait'
Face
Summer / Fall

모란
Tree peony
Paeonia x suffruticosa
'Kopper Kettle'
Face
Spring

산딸나무
Dogwood
Cornus kousa
Pink
Gesture / Filler
Spring

장미
Rose
Rosa
'Pink Majolica'
Filler
Year-round

장미
Rose
Rosa
'Emily'
Filler
Year-round

장미
Rose
Rosa
'Tango'
Face / Filler
Spring / Fall

라넌큘러스
Ranunculus
Ranunculua asiaticus
Double peach
Face / Filler
Winter / Spring

거베라
Gerbera daisy
Gerbera x hybrida
Apricot
Face / Gesture
Year-round

장미
Rose
Rosa
'Distant Drum'
Face / Filler
Sping / Fall

칼라	장미	패롯 튤립	호접란
Calla lily	Rose	Parrot tulip	Phalaenopsis orchid
Zantedeschia	*Rosa*	*Tulipa*	*Phalaenopsis hybrid*
'Kiwi Blush'	'Quicksand'	'Libretto Parrot'	Pale yellow and pink
Gesture	Filler	Gesture	Face / Filler / Gesture
Year-round	Year-round	Spring	Year-round
작약	장미	디기탈리스	라넌큘러스
Peony	Rose	Foxglove	Ranunculus
Paeonia lactiflora	*Rosa*	*Digitalis purpurea*	*Ranunculus asiaticus*
'Lady Gay'	'Secret Garden'	Pale pink	Double pink
Face	Filler	Gesture / Face	Face / Filler
Spring	Year-round	Spring / Summer	Winter / Spring
맨드라미	장미	카네이션	장미
Coxcomb	Rose	Carnation	Rose
Celosia cristata	*Rosa*	*Dianthus*	*Rosa*
Green and pale pink	'Caffe Latte'	Variegated	'Pink Raddish'
Filler	Face / Filler	Filler	Texture / Filler
Summer / Fall	Year-round	Year-round	Year-round
라일락	아킬레아	촛불 맨드라미	장미
Lilac	Yarrow	Celosia	Rose
Syringa vulgaris	*Achillea millefolium*	*Celosia spicata*	*Rosa*
'Beauty of Moscow'	Pink-purple	Pink-purple	'Amnesia'
Filler	Filler / Texture	Gesture / Texture	Filler
Spring	Year-round	Summer / Fall	Year-round
스위트피	델피니움	겹벚꽃	투베로사
Sweet pea	Larkspur	Cherry blossom	Tuberose
Lathyrus odoratus	*Consolida regalis*	*Prunus glandulosa*	*Polianthes tuberosa*
Lavender	Pale pink	'Sinensis' double pink	'Pink Sapphire'
Texture / Filler / Gesture	Filler / Texture	Gesture / Filler	Gesture
Winter / Spring	Year-round	Spring	Year-round

아가판서스
Agapanthus

Agapanthus praecox

Blue
Texture / Filler
Year-round

스타티스
Statice

Limonium sinuatum

Pale blue
Filler
Year-round

스카비오사
Scabiosa

Scabiosa caucasica

Pale blue
Gesture
Year-round

캄파눌라
Campanula / bellflower

Campanula medium

Pale blue
Filler
Spring / Summer

프리틸라리아
Fritilaria

Fritillaria hermonis

Green and brown
Gesture
Spring

알리움
Allium

Allium cepa

'Snake Ball'
Gesture
Spring

암소니아
Blue star

Amsonia tabernaemontana

Blue
Texture / Filler
Summer

니겔라
Nigella

Nigella damascena

Blue
Texture
Spring/ Summer

프리틸라리아
Fritillaria

Fritillaria persica

'Ivory Bells'
Face / Gesture
Spring

헬레보러스
Hellebore

Helleborus x hybridus

Double green and purple
Face / Filler
Winter / Spring

프리틸라리아
Fritillaria

Fritillaria pontica

Green and brown
Gesture
Spring

맨드라미
Coxcomb

Celosia cristata

Pale green
Filler
Summer / Fall

불두화
Viburnum

Viburnum opulus

'Roseum'
Filler
Spring

튤립
Tulip

Tulipa

'White Parrot'
Gesture
Spring

투베로사
Tuberose

Polianthes tuberosa

'The Pearl'
Gesture
Year-round

헬레보러스
Hellebore

Helleborus x hybridus

Green and cream
Face / Filler
Winter / Spring

알리움
Allium / Sicilian onion

Allium siculum

Cream and brown
Texture
Spring

헬레보러스
Hellebore

Helleborus x hybridus

Green and purple
Face / Filler
Winter / Spring

프렌치 패롯 튤립
French parrot tulip

Tulipa

Green
Gesture
Spring

라넌큘러스
Ranunculus

Ranunculus asiaticus

Double green
Face / Filler
Winter / Spring

수국
Hydrangea
Hydrangea macrophylla

Brown and pink
Filler
Year-round

헬레보러스
Hellebore / Christmas rose
Helleborus niger

Brown
Face / Filler
Winter / Spring

퀸앤스레이스
Queen Anne's lace
Daucus carota

'Dara'
Gesture / Texture
Summer / Fall

피어리스
Andromeda
Pieris japonica

White
Texture / Filler
Winter / Spring

캥커루발톱
Kangaroo paw
Anigozanthos

Pink and orange
Texture
Year-round

왁스 플라워
Wax flower
Chamelaucium uncinatum

Pink and white variegated
Texture / Filler
Year-round

장미
Rose
Rosa

'Koko Loko'
Face / Filler
Spring / Fall

에레무르스
Foxtail lily
Eremurus robustus

Peach
Gesture
Spring / Summer

장미
Rose
Rosa

'Golden Mustard'
Filler
Year-round

그레빌레아
Grevillea
Grevillea pteridifolia

Pale yellow
Gesture / Texture
Year-round

프리틸라리아
Snake's head fritillary
Fritillaria meleagris

Purple
Gesture / Texture
Spring

라넌큘러스
Ranunculus
Ranunculus asiaticus

Double white and brown
Face / Filler
Winter / Spring

부활절 백합
Easter lily
Lilium longiflorum

White
Face
Year-round

수선화
Narcissus
Narcissus

'Bridal Crown'
Filler
Winter / Spring

캐모마일
Chamomile
Matricaria chamomilla

White and yellow
Texture / Filler
Year-round

스카비오사
Scabiosa
Scabiosa atropurpurea

Pale cream
Gesture
Year-round

장미
Rose
Rosa

Crocus Rose 'Ausquest'
Face / Filler
Spring / Fall

파피오페딜럼
Lady's slipper orchid
Paphiopedilum

Yellow
Face
Year-round

소국
Daisy mum
Chrysanthemum

Hybrid yellow
Filler
Year-round

작약
Peony
Paeonia lactiflora

'Day Star'
Face
Spring

글로리오사 Gloriosa lily *Gloriosa superba* 'Lutea' Texture / Gesture Year-round	**수선화** Narcissus *Narcissus* 'Tahiti' Gesture / Filler Spring	**작약** Peony *Paeonia lactiflora* 'Lemon Dream' Face Spring	**작약** Peony *Paeonia lactiflora* 'Claire de Lune' Face Spring
프리지아 Freesia *Freesia* Double yellow Filler Year-round	**튤립** Tulip *Tulipa* 'Yellow Flight' Gesture Spring	**팬지** Pansy *Viola* hybrid Yellow Filler Winter / spring	**개나리** Forsythia *Forsythia x intermedia* Yellow Gesture / Texture Spring
프렌치 패롯 튤립 French parrot tulip *Tulipa* Yellow Gesture Spring	**버터플라이 라넌큘러스** Butterfly ranunculus *Ranunculus asiaticus* Yellow Gesture / Filler Winter / Spring	**거베라** Gerbera daisy *Gerbera x hybrida* Butter yellow Face Year-round	**튤립** Tulip *Tulipa* 'Monte Spider' Gesture Spring
미모사 Mimosa *Acacia retinodes* Yellow Filler / Texture Winter / Spring	**솔리다고** Goldenrod *Solidago canadensis* Yellow Filler / Texture Summer / Fall	**온시디움** Oncidium orchid *Oncidium* Hybrid yellow Filler / Gesture Year-round	**풍년화** Witch hazel *Hamamelis x intermedia* Yellow Gesture / Texture Winter / Spring
금잔화 Calendula *Calendula officinalis* Yellow Filler Spring / Summer	**아킬레아** Yarrow *Achillea filipendulina* Gold Filler / Texture Year-round	**수선화** Daffodil *Narcissus pseudonarcissus* Yellow Face Winter / Spring	**수선화** Narcissus *Narcissus* 'Soleil d'Or' Filler Winter / Spring

프렌치 튤립
French tulip
Tulipa

Yellow and red
Gesture
Spring

매리골드
French marigold
Tagetes patula

Striped mix
Texture / Gesture
Summer

해바라기
Sunflower
Helianthus annuus

Yellow
Face
Summer

라넌큘러스
Ranunculus
Ranunculus asiaticus

Clooney series, double yellow
Face / Filler
Winter / Spring

파피오페딜럼
Lady's slipper orchid
Paphiopedilum hybrid

Brown and green
Face
Year-round

스위트피
Sweet pea
Lathyrus odoratus

Yellow dyed
Texture / Filler / Gesture
Winter / Spring

맨드라미
Coxcomb
Celosia cristata

Yellow
Filler
Summer / Fall

온시디움
Oncidium orchid
Oncidium

Yellow
Gesture / Texture
Year-round

산더소니아
Golden lantern lily
Sandersonia aurantiaca

Orange
Gesture / Texture
Spring / Summer

버터플라이 라넌큘러스
Butterfly ranunculus
Ranunculus asiaticus

Single orange
Gesture / Filler
Winter / Spring

장미
Rose
Rosa

'Combo'
Filler
Year-round

백합
Lily
Lilium

'Solange'
Face
Year-round

글로리오사
Gloriosa lily
Gloriosa superba

Orange
Gesture
Year-round

아스클레피아스
Butterfly weed
Asclepias tuberosa

Orange
Filler / Texture
Year-round

달리아
Dahlia
Dahlia

'Lakeview Lucky'
Face / Filler
Summer / Fall

금잔화
Calendula
Calendula officinalis

'Indian Prince'
Filler
Spring / Summer

핀쿠션 프로테아
Pincushion protea
Leucospermum

'Carnival Orange'
Face / Texture
Year-round

라넌큘러스
Ranunculus
Ranunculus asiaticus

Gold and red variegated
Face / Filler
Winter / Spring

극락조
Birds of paradise
Strelitzia reginae

Orange
Face / Gesture
Year-round

수선화
Narcissus
Narcissus

'Johann Strauss'
Filler
Spring

프리틸라리아 Fritillaria *Fritillaria imperialis* Orange Face / Gesture Spring	**오니소갈럼** Orange chincherinchee *Ornithogalum dubium* Orange Filler Year-round	**라넌큘러스** Ranunculus *Ranunculus asiaticus* Double orange Face / Filler Winter / Spring	**에피덴드룸** Epidendrum *Epidendrum* hybrid Orange Face / Gesture Year-round
천일홍 Gomphrena *Gomphrena globosa* Orange Filler Summer / Fall	**라넌큘러스** Ranunculus *Ranunculus asiaticus* Clooney series, peach Face / Filler Winter / Spring	**장미** Rose *Rosa* Renaissance series 'Claire' Face / Filler Spring / Fall	**아이슬란드 양귀비** Icelandic poppy *Papaver nudicaule* Peach Face / Gesture Winter / Spring
프렌치 튤립 French tulip *Tulipa* 'Flaming Parrot' Gesture Spring	**말나리 계** Martagon hybrid *Lilium x martagon* 'Orange Marmalade' Gesture / Texture Summer	**칼라** Calla lily *Zantedeschia* 'Mango' Gesture / Filler Year-round	**안수리움** Anthurium *Anthurium* 'Rothschildianum' Face Year-round
맨드라미 Plumosa celosia *Celosia argentea* Rust Filler / Texture Summer / Fall	**헬리코니아** Heliconia *Heliconia stricta* Red Face Year-round	**아이슬란드 양귀비** Icelandic poppy *Papaver nudicaule* Orange Gesture / Face Winter / Spring	**달리아** Dahlia *Dahlia* 'Iced Tea' Face / Filler Summer / Fall
안수리움 Anthurium *Anthurium* 'Hawaii' Face Year-round	**장미** Rose *Rosa* 'Toffee' Filler Year-round	**국화** Spider mum *Chrysanthemum* Orange and yellow Face / Filler Fall	**튤립** Tulip *Tulipa* 'Leo' Gesture Spring

제임스 스토리 James Story orchid *Oncidium* hybrid Yellow and brown Gesture / Texture Year-round	온시디움 Oncidium orchid *Oncidium* hybrid Orange and brown Gesture / Texture Year-round	국화 Spider mum *Chrysanthemum* 'Seaton's Toffee' Face / Filler Fall	맨드라미 Coxcomb *Celosia cristata* Rust Filler Summer / Fall
라넌큘러스 Ranunculus *Ranunculus asiaticus* 'Charlotte' peach Face Winter / Spring	스위트피 Sweet pea *Lathyrus odoratus* Brown dyed Texture / Filler / Gesture Winter / Spring	사라세니아 Pitcher plant *Sarracenia leucophylla* Red and white variegated Texture Spring / Summer	아마릴리스 Amaryllis *Hippeastrum cybister* 'Tarantula' Face Winter
달리아 Dahlia *Dahlia* 'Gitts Crazy' Face Summer / Fall	달리아 Dahlia *Dahlia* 'Cornel Bronze' Face / Filler Summer / Fall	달리아 Dahlia *Dahlia* 'Bahama Apricot' Face Summer / Fall	독일붓꽃 Beared iris *Iris germanica* Purple and brown Face Spring
아마릴리스 Amaryllis *Hippeastrum* 'Rilona' Face Winter	장미 Rose *Rosa* 'Kahala' Filler Year-round	모란 Tree peony *Paeonia x suffruticosa* 'Callie's Memory' Face Spring	안수리움 Anthurium *Anthurium* 'Cognac' Face Year-round
아이슬란드 양귀비 Icelandic poppy *Papaver nudicaule* Watermelon Face / Gesture Winter / Spring	산당화 Quince *Chaenomeles japonica* Coral Gesture Winter / Spring	백일홍 Zinnia *Zinnia elegans* Coral Face / Filler Summer	산당화 Quince *Chaenomeles speciosa* Red Gesture Winter / Spring

카네이션 Carnation *Dianthus* Pink and red Filler Year-round	**달리아** Dahlia *Dahlia* Pale red Face / Filler Summer / Fall	**크리스마스 부쉬** Christmas bush *Ceratopetalum gummiferum* 'Albery's Red' Texture / Filler Fall / Winter	**달리아** Dahlia *Dahlia* 'Amber Queen' Face / Filler Summer / Fall
프렌치 튤립 French tulip *Tulipa* 'Kingsblood' Gesture Spring	**달리아** Dahlia *Dahlia* 'Red and White Fubuki' Face Summer / Fall	**버터플라이 라넌큘러스** Butterfly ranunculus *Ranunculus asiaticus* Double rust Gesture / Filler Winter / Spring	**코스모스** Cosmos *Cosmos atrosanguineus* Dark red Gesture Summer / Fall
거베라 Gerbera daisy *Gerbera x hybrida* Red Facc Year-round	**틸란시아** Quill *Tillandsia cyanea hybrid* Red Filler Year-round	**아마릴리스** Amaryllis *Hippeastrum* 'Simply Red' Face Winter	**헬리코니아** Heliconia *Heliconia vellerigera* 'King Kong' Face Year-round
스프레이 카네이션 Spray carnation *Dianthus* 'Solomio Amos' Texture / Filler Year-round	**프렌치 패롯 튤립** French parrot tulip *Tulipa* 'Red Parrot' Gesture Spring	**시클라멘** Cyclamen *Cyclamen persicum* Red Filler Spring	**안수리움** Anthurium *Anthurium andraeanum* Red Face Year-round
맨드라미 Coxcomb *Celosia cristata* Dark red Filler Summer / Fall	**라넌큘러스** Ranunculus *Ranunculus asiaticus* Dark red Face / Filler Winter / Spring	**아네모네** Anemone *Anemone coronaria* Red Face Winter / Spring	**백일홍** Zinnia *Zinnia elegans* Double red Face / Filler Summer

튤립 Tulip *Tulipa* 'Black Hero' Gesture Spring	**장미** Rose *Rosa* Black Magic 'Tankalcig' Filler Year-round	**달리아** Dahlia *Dahlia* Dark red Face Summer / Fall	**장미** Rose *Rosa* 'Red Piano' Face / Filler Year-round
종이꽃 Straw flower *Xerochrysum bracteatum* Burgundy Filler / Texture Summer / Fall	**작약** Peony *Paeonia lactiflora* 'Chocolate Soldier' Face Spring	**작약** Peony *Paeonia lactiflora* 'Black Swan' Face Spring	**라넌큘러스** Ranunculus *Ranunculus asiaticus* Red and brown variegated Face / Filler Winter / Spring
리시안셔스 Lisianthus *Eustoma russellianum* Brown and purple variegated Filler Year-round	**심비디움** Cymbidium orchid *Cymbidium hybrid* Dark pink Face / Gesture Year-round	**수국** Hydrangea *Hydrangea macrophylla* Dark pink Filler Year-round	**아스틸베** Astilbe *Astilbe* 'Red Sentinel' Texture Year-round
달리아 Dahlia *Dahlia* 'Sonic Bloom' Face Summer / Fall	**아네모네** Anenome *Anemone coronaria* Red and white variegated Face Winter / Spring	**라넌큘러스** Ranunculus *Ranunculus asiaticus* Dark pink Face / Filler Winter / Spring	**모란** Tree peony *Paeonia x suffruticosa* Dark pink and peach Face Spring
장미 Rose *Rosa* 'Pink Piano' Face / Filler Year-round	**진달래** Azalea *Rhododendron molle* Pink hybrid Filler Spring	**스위트피** Sweet pea *Lathyrus odoratus* Red Texture / Filler / Gesture Winter / Spring	**알피니아** Ginger *Alpinia purpurata* Red Face Year-round

라넌큘러스 Ranunculus *Ranunculus asiaticus* Double pink and green Face / Filler Winter / Spring	**스위트피** Sweet pea *Lathyrus odoratus* Coral Texture / Filler / Gesture Winter / Spring	**장미** Rose *Rosa* 'Pink Floyd' Filler Year-round	**장미** Rose *Rosa* Kate 'Auschris' Face / Filler Spring / Fall
장미 Rose *Rosa* 'Romantic Antike' Face / Filler Year-round	**와라타** Waratah *Telopea speciosissima* Pink Face / Texture Summer / Fall	**장미** Rose *Rosa* Benjamin Britten 'Ausencart' Face / Filler Spring / Fall	**작약** Peony *Paeonia* 'Coral Charm' Face Spring
라넌큘러스 Ranunculus *Ranunculus asiaticus* Double pink Face / Filler Winter / Spring	**장미** Rose *Rosa* 'Lady Moon' Filler Year-round	**작약** Peony *Paeonia lactiflora* 'Dr Alexander Fleming' Face Spring	**안수리움** Anthurium *Anthurium* 'Marea' Face Year-round
금낭화 Bleeding heart *Lamprocapnos* *spectabilis* Pink Gesture / Texture Spring	**스타티스** Statice *Limonium sinuatum* Pink Filler Year-round	**리시안셔스** Lisianthus *Eustoma russellianum* Double pink Filler Year-round	**프렌치 튤립** French tulip *Tulipa* Pink Gesture Spring
수련 Water lily *Nymphaea* Pink Face Year-round	**라넌큘러스** Ranunculus *Ranunculus asiaticus* 'Charlotte' burgundy and white Face Winter / Spring	**작약** Peony *Paeonia lactiflora* 'Nymphe' Face Spring	**달리아** Dahlia *Dahlia* 'Lagoon' Face Summer / Fall

라넌큘러스
Ranunculus

Ranunculus asiaticus

Clooney series, pale pink
Face / Filler
Winter / Spring

작약
Peony

Paeonia lactiflora

'Sarah Bernhardt'
Face
Spring

스카비오사
Scabiosa

Scabiosa columbaria

Pink
Gesture
Year-round

에키네시아
Echinacea

Echinacea purpurea

Pink
Face / Filler
Summer

아네모네
Anemone

Anemone coronaria

Double magenta
Face
Winter / Spring

장미
Rose

Rosa

'Royal Amethyst'
Face / Filler
Spring / Fall

목련
Magnolia

Magnolia x soulangeana

'Alexandrina'
Face / Gesture
Spring

매화나무
Plum blossom

Prunus mume

Pink
Gesture
Spring

헬레보러스
Hellebore

Helleborus x hybridus

Dark pink
Face / Filler
Winter

거베라
Gerbera daisy

Gerbera x hybrida

Double dark pink
Face
Year-round

추명국
Autumn anemone / Japanese anemone

Anemone hupehensis

Pale purple
Gesture
Fall

불로초
Sedum

Hylotelephium telephium

Pink
Filler
Summer / Fall

스위트피
Sweet pea

Lathyrus odoratus

Purple and white variegated
Texture / Filler / Gesture
Winter / Spring

디기탈리스
Foxglove

Digitalis purpurea

Purple
Gesture / Face
Spring / Summer

그레빌레아
Grevillea

Grevillea

'Robyn Gordon'
Gesture / Texture
Year-round

백일홍
Zinnia

Zinnia elegans

'Queen Lime Blush'
Filler
Summer

시레네
Sweet William catchfly

Silene armeria

Purple
Texture / Filler
Spring

보로니아
Boronia

Boronia heterophylla

Purple
Filler / Texture
Spring

달리아
Dahlia

Dahlia

'Koko Puff'
Face / Filler
Summer / Fall

헤더
Heather

Calluna vulgaris

Dark pink
Texture / Filler
Year-round

장미
Rose
Rosa

'Menta'
Filler
Year-round

국화
Chrysanthemum
Chrysanthemum

Lilac
Filler
Year-round

달리아
Dahlia
Dahlia

'Mikayla Miranda'
Face
Summer / Fall

안수리움
Anthurium
Anthurium

'Previa'
Face
Year-round

리아트리스
Liatris
Liatris spicata

Purple
Gesture
Year-round

델피니움
Delphinium
Delphinium

Lavender
Gesture / Face
Year-round

패롯 튤립
Parrot tulip
Tulipa

'Blue Parrot'
Gesture
Spring

스위트피
Sweet pea
Lathyrus odoratus

'Matucana'
Texture / Filler / Gesture
Winter / Spring

스위트피
Sweet pea
Lathyrus odoratus

Chocolate dyed
Texture / Filler / Gesture
Winter / Spring

독일붓꽃
Bearded iris
Iris germanica

'Indian Chief'
Face
Spring

아스트란시아
Astrantia
Astrantia major

'Rosensinfonie'
Texture / Filler
Year-round

라넌큘러스
Ranunculus
Ranunculus asiaticus

Purple and mauve variegated
Face / Filler
Winter / Spring

라일락
Lilac
Syringa

Lavender
Texture / Filler
Spring

알리움
Allium
Allium cepa

Purple and gray
Gesture
Spring

헬레보러스
Hellebore
Helleborus x hybridus

Dark purple
Face / Filler
Winter / Spring

리시안셔스
Lisianthus
Eustoma russellianum

Dark purple
Filler
Year-round

클레마티스
Clematis
Clematis alpina

'Tage Lundell' lavender
Gesture / Filler
Year-round

루피너스
Lupine
Lupinus x regalis

Blue
Gesture
Spring / Summer

스위트피
Sweet pea
Lathyrus odoratus

'Chocolate Flake'
Texture / Filler / Gesture
Winter / Spring

온시디움
Oncidium orchid
Oncidium hybrid

'Kauai'
Gesture
Year-round

스위트피 Sweet pea *Lathyrus nervosus* Purple Texture / Filler / Gesture Winter / Spring	**캥거루발톱** Kangaroo paw *Anigozanthos flavidus* 'Ember' purple variegated Gesture / Texture Year-round	**벨 클레마티스** Bell clematis *Clematis* 'Rooguchi' purple Gesture Spring	**헬레보러스** Hellebore *Helleborus × hybridus* Double pink and white variegated Face / Filler Winter / Spring
아네모네 Anemone *Anemone coronaria* Lavender Face Winter / Spring	**수련** Water lily *Nymphaea nouchali* Lavender Face Year-round	**시네라리아** Cineraria *Pericallis × hybrida* Blue Texture / Filler Spring	**벨 클레마티스** Bell clematis *Clematis* 'Rooguchi' blue Gesture Spring
과꽃 China aster *Callistephus chinensis* Double blue Filler Summer	**베로니카** Veronica *Veronica longifolia* Purple Gesture Year-round	**클레마티스** Clematis *Clematis lanuginosa* Purple Face Year-round	**아게라텀** Floss flower *Ageratum houstonianum* Purple Filler Summer
물망초 Forget-me-not *Myosotis sylvatica* Blue Gesture Winter / Spring	**히아신스** Hyacinth *Hyacinthus orientalis* 'Delft Blue' Filler Spring	**수국** Hydrangea *Hydrangea macrophylla* Pale purple variegated Filler Year-round	**라벤더** Lavender *Lavandula × intermedia* Lavender Gesture / Texture Year-round
옥시페탈룸 Tweedia *Tweedia caerulea* Blue Filler Year-round	**알리움** Allium *Allium caeruleum* Blue Gesture Spring	**무스카리** Muscari *Muscari botryoides* Blue Gesture / Texture Winter / Spring	**델피니움** Larkspur *Consolida regalis* Pale blue Gesture / Texture Year-round

델피니움
Delphinium

Delphinium

Blue
Gesture / Face
Year-round

에린기움
Blue thistle

Eryngium planum

Blue
Texture
Year-round

아이리스
Iris

Iris latifolia

Blue
Gesture / Filler
Spring

수레국화
Cornflower

Centaurea cyanus

Blue
Gesture / Filler
Spring

독일붓꽃
Bearded iris

Iris germanica

'Black Knight'
Face
Spring

서양매발톱꽃
Columbine

Aquilegia vulgaris var. *stellata*

'Black Barlow'
Gesture / Texture
Summer

미니 델피니움
Larkspur

Consolida regalis

Dark blue
Gesture / Texture
Year-round

수국
Hydrangea

Hydrangea macrophylla

Blue
Filler
Year-round

작약
Peony

Paeonia lactiflora

'Black Panther'
Face
Spring

거베라
Gerbera daisy

Gerbera x hybrida

Dark red
Face / Filler
Year-round

모란
Tree peony

Paeonia x suffruticosa

'Vesuvian'
Face
Spring

스카비오사
Scabiosa

Scabiosa atropurpurea

Dark red
Gesture
Year-round

촛불 맨드라미
Plumosa celosia

Celosia argentea

Dark red
Texture / Filler
Summer / Fall

모란
Tree peony

Paeonia x suffruticosa

'Burgundy Wine'
Face
Spring

파피오페딜럼
Lady's slipper orchid

Paphiopedilum

Burgundy
Face
Year-round

스프레이 카네이션
Spray carnation

Dianthus

Pink and purple variegated
Texture / Filler
Year-round

말나리 계
Martagon hybrid

Lilium x dalhansonii

Dark red
Gesture / Texture
Year-round

패롯 튤립
Parrot tulip

Tulipa

'Rococo'
Gesture
Spring

장미
Rose

Rosa

'Flash Night'
Filler
Year-round

코스모스
Cosmos

Cosmos bipinnatus

'Rubenza'
Gesture
Summer

프리틸라리아 Fritillaria *Fritillaria uva-vulpis* Brown and yellow Gesture Spring	**심비디움** Cymbidium orchid *Cymbidium hybrid* Brown Face / Gesture Year-round	**튤립** Tulip *Tulipa* Brown Gesture Spring	**백일홍** Zinnia *Zinnia elegans* Persian carpet mix Texture / Filler Summer / Fall
튤립 Tulip *Tulipa* 'Black Jack' Gesture Spring	**카네이션** Carnation *Dianthus* Dark purple Filler Year-round	**칼라** Calla lily *Zantedeschia* 'Red Star' Gesture / Filler Year-round	**사라세니아** Pitcher plant *Sarracenia x moorei* Dark burgundy Texture Summer
달리아 Dahlia *Dahlia* 'Kokucho' Face Fall	**프리틸라리아** Fritillaria *Fritillaria persica* Dark purple Face / Gesture Winter / Spring	**해바라기** Sunflower *Helianthus annuus* 'Black Beauty' Face Summer	**루드베키아** Black eyed Susan *Rudbeckia hirta* 'Cherry Brandy' Face / Filler Summer
코스모스 Cosmos *Cosmos atrosanguineus* 'Chocamocha' Gesture Summer / Fall	**라넌큘러스** Ranunculus *Ranunculus asiaticus* Black Face / Filler Winter / Spring	**달리아** Dahlia *Dahlia* 'Karma Choc' Face Summer / Fall	**달리아** Dahlia *Dahlia* 'Crossfield Ebony' Face / Filler Summer / Fall
칼라 Calla lily *Zantedeschia* 'Black Star' Gesture Year-round	**스카비오사** Scabiosa *Scabiosa atropurpurea* Black Gesture Year-round	**안수리움** Anthurium *Anthurium* 'Karma Black' Face Year-round	**헬레보러스** Hellebore *Helleborus x hybridus* Double black Face / Filler Winter / Spring

식물학명 색인

A

Acacia retinodes, 191, 453
Achillea filipendulina, 194, 453
Achillea millefolium, 130, 447
Actinotus helianthi, 24, 437
Agapanthus praecox, 139, 449
Ageratum houstonianum, 364, 471
Allium caeruleum, 374, 471
Allium cepa, 350, 469
  'Snake Ball', 142, 449
Allium neapolitanum, 28, 437
Allium siculum, 155, 449
Alpinia purpurata, 292, 463
Amsonia tabernaemontana, 141, 449
Anemone
  Anemone coronaria 33, 273, 290, 323, 363, 437, 461, 463, 467, 471
  De Caen Group white, 35, 437
  Anemone hupehensis, 325, 467
Anigozanthos, 163, 451
  'Bush Diamond', 21, 437
  'Ember', 358, 471
Anthurium
  'Acropolis', 65, 441
  'Cognac', 248, 459
  'Hawaii', 235, 457
  'Karma Black', 413, 475
  'Lumina', 71, 441
  'Marea', 304, 465
  'Previa', 336, 469
  'Rothschildianum', 224, 457
  Anthurium andraeanum, 268, 461
Aquilegia vulgaris var. *stellata* 'Black Barlow', 382, 473
Asclepias tuberosa, 210, 455
Astilbe
  'Deutschland', 61, 441
  'Elizabeth Bloom'', 90, 443
  'Red Sentinel', 284, 463
Astrantia major
  'Rosensinfonie', 345, 469
  'White Giant', 42, 439

B

Boronia heterophylla, 334, 467

C

Calendula officinalis 195, 453
  'Indian Prince', 208, 455
Callistephus chinensis, 367, 471
Calluna vulgaris, 332, 467
Campanula medium, 136, 449
Celosia argentea, 231, 391, 457, 473
Celosia cristata, 127, 144, 201, 236, 275, 447, 449, 455, 459, 461
Celosia spicata, 129, 447
Centaurea cyanus, 376, 473
Ceratopetalum gummiferum 'Albery's Red', 257, 461
Chaenomeles japonica, 254, 459
Chaenomeles speciosa, 252, 459
  'Nivalis', 72, 441
Chamelaucium uncinatum, 73, 162, 441, 451
Chrysanthemum, 173, 233, 338, 451, 457, 469
  'Seaton's Je Dore', 93, 443
  'Seaton's Toffee', 237, 459
Clematis
  'Rooguchi', 357, 360, 471
  Clematis alpina 'Tage Lundell', 355, 469
  Clematis lanuginosa, 365, 471
Consolida regalis, 134, 372, 381, 447, 471, 473
Convallaria majalis, 52, 439
Cornus kousa, 110, 445
  var. *chinensis*, 82, 443
Cosmos atrosanguineus, 260, 461
  'Chocamocha', 411, 475
Cosmos bipinnatus, 67, 441
  'Rubenza', 392, 473
Cyclamen persicum 17, 269, 437, 461
Cymbidium hybrid, 286, 398, 463, 475

D

Dahlia, 44, 92, 209, 228, 247, 256, 258, 277, 291, 312, 333, 337, 439, 443, 455, 457, 459, 461, 463, 465, 467, 469
  'Amber Queen', 256, 461
  'Bahama Apricot', 245, 459
  'Cafe au Lait', 104, 445
  'Cornel Bronze', 246, 459
  'Cream and Pink', 92, 443
  'Crossfield Ebony', 408, 475
  'Figaro', 66, 441
  'Gitts Crazy', 247, 459
  'Iced Tea', 228, 457
  'Karma Choc', 409, 475
  'Koko Puff', 333, 467
  'Kokucho', 407, 475

'Lagoon', 312, 465
'Lakeview Lucky', 209, 455
'Mikayla Miranda', 337, 469
'Red and White Fubuki', 262, 461
'Sonic Bloom', 291, 463
Daucus carota 'Dara', 157, 451
Delphinium, 342, 379, 469, 473
'Centurion White', 25, 437
Dianthus, 103, 125, 259, 388, 402, 445, 447, 461, 473, 475
'Grenadin White', 30, 437
'Solomio Amos', 271, 461
'Star Snow Tessino', 38, 439
Digitalis purpurea, 121, 330, 447, 467
f. albiflora, 83, 443

E

Echinacea purpurea, 316, 467
Epidendrum hybrid, 94, 216, 443, 457
Eremurus robustus, 160, 451
Eryngium planum, 378, 473
Eustoma russellianum, 56, 106, 287, 309, 348, 441, 445, 463, 465, 469

F

Forsythia x *intermedia*, 180, 453
Freesia, 47, 183, 439, 453
Fritillaria hermonis, 143, 449
Fritillaria imperialis, 219, 457
Fritillaria meleagris, 165, 451
Fritillaria persica, 406, 475
'Ivory Bells', 147, 449
Fritillaria pontica, 145, 449
Fritillaria uva-vulpis, 399, 475

G

Gerbera x *hybrida*, 57, 113, 185, 267, 326, 386, 441, 445, 453, 461, 467, 473
Gladiolus
'The Bride', 62, 441
'White Prosperity', 46, 439
Gladiolus x *convillii* 'Albus', 45, 439
Gloriosa superba, 211, 455
'Lutea', 179, 453
Gomphrena globosa, 223, 457
Grevillea
'Robyn Gordon', 329, 467
Grevillea pteridifolia, 166, 451

H

Hamamelis x *intermedia*, 188, 453

Helianthus annuus, 197, 455
'Black Beauty', 405, 475
Heliconia stricta, 230, 457
Heliconia vellerigera 'King Kong', 264, 461
Helleborus niger, 158, 451
Helleborus x *hybridus*, 146, 148, 154, 327, 349, 356, 412, 449, 467, 469, 471, 475
Hippeastrum
'Rilona', 251, 459
'Simply Red', 265, 461
'White Dazzler', 40, 439
Hippeastrum cybister
'Tarantula', 240, 459
Hyacinthus orientalis, 50, 91, 439, 443
'Delft Blue', 370, 471
Hydrangea macrophylla, 159, 285, 369, 380, 451, 463, 471, 473
'White Swan', 18, 437
Hylotelephium telephium, 324, 467

I

Iris germanica, 244, 459
'Black Knight', 383, 473
'Indian Chief', 346, 469
'Party Dress', 97, 445
Iris latifolia, 377, 473

J

Jasminum polyanthum, 86, 443

L

Lamprocapnos spectabilis, 311, 465
Lathyrus latifolius 'Albus', 60, 441
Lathyrus nervosus, 359, 471
Lathyrus odoratus, 58, 78, 135, 202, 242, 293, 298, 331, 347, 353, 441, 443, 447, 455, 459, 463, 465, 467, 469
'Matucana', 340, 469
Lavandula x *intermedia*, 368, 471
Leucojum aestivum, 59, 441
Leucospermum 'Carnival Orange', 215, 455
Liatris spicata, 343, 469
Lilium, 88, 107, 443, 445
'Orange Marmalade', 226, 457
'Premium Blond', 29, 437
'Solange', 204, 455
Lilium longiflorum, 171, 451
Lilium x *dalhansonii*, 395, 473
Limonium sinuatum, 98, 138, 310, 445, 449, 465
Lupinus x *regalis*, 354, 469
Lysimachia clethroides, 55, 439

M

Magnolia x soulangeana 'Alexandrina', 321, 467
Matricaria chamomilla, 169, 451
Matthiola incana, 22, 89, 101, 437, 443, 445
Muscari azureum 'Album', 54, 439
Muscari botryoides, 373, 471
Myosotis sylvatica, 371, 471

N

Narcissus
    'Bridal Crown', 170, 451
    'Johann Strauss', 212, 455
    'Salome', 87, 443
    'Soleil d'Or', 192, 453
    'Tahiti', 178, 453
Narcissus papyraceus, 26, 437
Narcissus poeticus hybrid, 48, 439
Narcissus pseudonarcissus, 193, 453
Nerine bowdenii 'Pallida', 32, 437
Nigella damascena, 68, 140, 441, 449
Nymphaea alba, 315, 465
Nymphaea nouchali, 362, 471

O

Oncidium 200, 455
    hybrid 81, 189, 238, 239, 443, 453, 459
    hybrid 'Kauai', 352, 469
Ornithogalum dubium, 218, 457

P

Paeonia
    'Bowl of Cream', 39, 439
    'Coral Charm', 300, 465
Paeonia lactiflora
    'Black Panther', 387, 473
    'Black Swan', 281, 463   'Chocolate Soldier', 282, 463
    'Claire de Lune', 176, 453
    'Day Star', 172, 451
    'Dr Alexander Fleming', 305, 465
    'Duchesse de Nemours', 79, 443
    'Festiva Maxima', 70, 441
    'Lady Gay', 123, 447 'Lemon Dream', 177, 453
    'Nymphe', 313, 465
    'Rooster Reveille', 77, 443
    'Sarah Bernhardt', 318, 467
    'Sonata', 76, 443
Paeonia x suffruticosa, 288, 463
    'Burgundy Wine', 390, 473
    'Callie's Memory', 249, 459
    'Kopper Kettle', 111, 445
    'Vesuvian', 385, 473
Papaver nudicaule, 220, 229, 255, 457, 459
Paphiopedilum, 174, 389, 451, 473
    hybrid, 203, 455
Pericallis x hybrida, 361, 471
Phalaenopsis hybrid, 116, 447
Pieris japonica, 156, 451
Pimelea phylicoides, 74, 441
Polianthes tuberosa
    'Pink Sapphire', 132, 447
    'The Pearl', 149, 449
Polygonatum biflorum, 53, 439
Prunus glandulosa 'Sinensis', 133, 447
Prunus mume pink, 320, 467
Prunus x subhirtella 'Autumnalis', 20, 437

R

Ranunculus asiaticus 23, 114, 120, 152, 164, 186, 206, 214, 217, 261, 274, 280, 289, 299, 307, 344, 410, 437, 445, 447, 449, 451, 453, 455, 457, 461, 463, 465, 469, 475
    'Butterfly Lux', 80, 443
    'Charlotte', 243, 314, 459, 465
    Clooney series 196, 222, 319, 455, 457, 467
Rhododendron molle hybrid, 16, 294, 437, 463
Rosa
    'Amnesia', 128, 447
    'Caffe Latte', 126, 447
    'Cappuccino', 100, 445
    'Combo', 205, 455
    'Champagne', 84, 443
    'Charity', 85, 443
    'Distant Drum', 112, 445
    'Emily', 108, 445
    'Flash Night', 393, 473
    'Garden Snow', 51, 439
    'Golden Mustard', 167, 451
    'Kahala', 250, 459
    'Koko Loko', 161, 451
    'Lady Moon', 306, 465
    'Menta', 339, 469
    'Pink Floyd', 297, 465
    'Pink Majolica', 109, 445
    'Pink Piano', 295, 463
    'Pink Raddish', 124, 447
    'Quicksand', 118, 447
    'Red Piano', 276, 463
    'Romantic Antike', 303, 465
    'Royal Amethyst', 322, 467
    'Sahara', 95, 443
    'Sahara Sensation', 102, 445

'Secret Garden', 122, 447
'Tango', 115, 445
'Tibet', 27, 437
'Toffee', 234, 457
'White Majolica', 37, 439
Benjamin Britten 'Ausencart', 301, 465
Black Magic 'Tankalcig', 278, 463
Crocus Rose 'Ausquest', 175, 451
Juliet 'Ausjameson', 105, 445
Kate 'Auschris', 296, 465
Renaissance series 'Claire', 221, 457
Winchester Cathedral
'Auscat', 36, 439
Rudbeckia hirta 'Cherry Brandy', 404, 475

S

Sandersonia aurantiaca, 207, 455
Sarracenia leucophylla, 241, 459
Sarracenia x moorei, 400, 475
Scabiosa atropurpurea, 168, 384, 414, 451, 473, 475
Scabiosa caucasica, 137, 449
Scabiosa columbaria, 31, 317, 437, 467
Silene armeria, 335, 467
Solidago canadensis, 190, 453
Spiraea
'Arguta', 34, 437
Spiraea thunbergii, 75, 441
Strelitzia reginae, 213, 455
Syringa, 351, 469
Syringa vulgaris, 43, 439
'Beauty of Moscow', 131, 447

T

Tagetes patula, 198, 455
Telopea speciosissima, 302, 465
Tillandsia cyanea hybrid red inflorescence, 266, 461
Trachymene coerulea 'Lacy Pink', 69, 441
Tulipa, 153, 187, 199, 308, 397, 449, 453, 455, 465, 475
'Apricot Beauty', 96, 445
'Black Hero', 279, 463
'Black Jack', 403, 475
'Blue Parrot', 341, 469
'Flaming Parrot', 227, 457
'Honeymoon', 63, 441
'Kingsblood', 263, 461
'Leo', 232, 457
'Libretto Parrot', 117, 447
'Monte Spider', 184, 453
'Red Parrot', 270, 461
'Rococo', 394, 473
'White Liberstar', 49, 439
'White Parrot', 150, 449
'Yellow Flight', 182, 453
Tweedia caerulea, 375, 471
'Pint White', 19, 437

V

Veronica longifolia, 366, 471
Viburnum opulus 'Roseum', 151, 449
Viola hybrid 99, 181, 445, 453

X

Xerochrysum bracteatum, 283, 463

Z

Zantedeschia
'Aspen', 64, 441
'Black Star', 415, 475
'Kiwi Blush', 119, 447
'Mango', 225, 457
'Red Star', 401, 475
Zantedeschia aethiopica, 41, 439
Zinnia elegans, 253, 272, 459, 461
'Queen Lime Blush', 328, 396, 467, 475

보통명 색인

A
Agapanthus, 139, 449
Allium, 28, 142, 155, 350, 374, 437, 449, 469, 471
Amaryllis, 40, 240, 251, 265, 439, 459, 461
Andromeda, 156, 451
Anemone, 33, 35, 273, 290, 323, 363, 437, 461, 463, 467, 471
    Autumn anemone (*also* Japanese anemone), 325, 467
Anthurium, 65, 71, 224, 235, 248, 268, 304, 336, 413, 441, 457, 459, 461, 465, 469, 475
Astilbe, 61, 90, 284, 441, 443, 463
Astrantia, 42, 345, 439, 469
Autumn anemone, 325, 467
Azalea, 16, 294, 437, 463

B
Bearded iris, 97, 244, 346, 383, 445, 459, 469, 473
Bell clematis, 357, 360, 471
Birds of paradise, 213, 455
Black Eyed Susan, 404, 475
Bleeding heart, 311, 465
Blue lace flower, 69, 441
Blue Star, 141, 449
Blue thistle, 378, 473
Boronia, 334, 467
Butterfly ranunculus, 80, 186, 206, 261, 443, 453, 455, 461
Butterfly weed, 210, 455

C
Calendula, 195, 208, 453, 455
Calla lily, 41, 64, 119, 225, 401, 415, 439, 441, 447, 457, 475
Campanula / bellflower, 136, 449
Carnation, 103, 125, 259, 402, 445, 447, 461, 473, 475
    Spray carnation, 30, 38, 271, 388, 437, 439, 461, 473
Celosia, 129, 447
Chamomile, 169, 451
Cherry blossom, 133, 447
    Flowering cherry, 20, 437
China aster, 367, 471
Christmas bush, 257, 461
Christmas rose, 158, 451
Chrysanthemum, 93, 173, 338, 443, 451, 469
    Daisy mum, 173, 451
    Spider mum, 233, 237, 457, 459

Cineraria, 361, 471
Clematis, 355, 365, 469, 471
    Bell clematis, 357, 360, 471
Columbine, 382, 473
Cornflower, 376, 473
Cosmos, 67, 260, 392, 411, 441, 461, 473, 475
Coxcomb, 127, 144, 201, 236, 275, 447, 449, 455, 459, 461
Cyclamen, 17, 269, 437, 461
Cymbidium orchid, 286, 398, 463, 475

D
Daffodil, 193, 453
Dahlia, 44, 66, 92, 104, 209, 228, 245, 246, 247, 256, 258, 262, 277, 291, 312, 333, 337, 407, 439, 441, 443, 445, 455, 457, 459, 461, 463, 465, 467, 469, 475
Daisy mum, 173, 451
Delphinium, 342, 379, 469, 473
Dogwood, 82, 110, 443, 445

E
Easter lily, 171, 451
Echinacea, 316, 467
Epidendrum, 94, 216, 443, 457
Everlasting pea, 60, 441

F
Flannel flower, 24, 437
Floss flower, 364, 471
Flowering cherry, 20, 437
Forget-me-not, 371, 471
Forsythia, 180, 453
Foxglove, 83, 121, 330, 443, 447, 467
Foxtail lily, 160, 451
Freesia, 47, 183, 439, 453
French marigold, 198, 455
French parrot tulip, 153, 227, 270, 449, 457, 461
French tulip, 199, 263, 308, 455, 461, 465
Fritillaria, 143, 145, 147, 219, 399, 406, 449, 457, 475
    Snake's head fritillary, 165, 451

G
Gerbera daisy, 57, 113, 185, 267, 326, 386, 441, 445, 453, 461, 467, 473
Ginger, 292, 463
Gladiolus, 45, 46, 62, 439, 441
Gloriosa lily, 179, 211, 453, 455
Golden lantern lily, 207, 455

Goldenrod, 190, 453
Gomphrena, 223, 457
Gooseneck loosestrife, 55, 439
Grevillea, 166, 329, 451, 467

H
Heath rice flower, 74, 441
Heather, 332, 467
Heliconia, 230, 264, 457, 461
Hellebore, 146, 148, 154, 158, 327, 349, 356, 412, 449, 451, 467, 469, 471, 475
Hyacinth, 50, 91, 370, 439, 443, 471
Hydrangea, 18, 159, 285, 369, 380, 437, 451, 463, 471, 473

I
Icelandic Poppy, 220, 229, 255, 457, 459
Iris, 377, 473
    Bearded iris, 97, 244, 346, 383, 445, 459, 469, 473

J
Japanese anemone 325, 467
James Story orchid, 239, 459
Jasmine, 86, 443

K
Kangaroo paw, 21, 163, 358, 437, 451, 471

L
Lady's slipper orchid, 174, 203, 389, 451, 455, 473
Larkspur, 25, 134, 372, 379, 381, 437, 447, 469, 471, 473
Lavender, 368, 471
Liatris, 343, 469
Lilac, 43, 131, 351, 439, 447, 469
Lily, 29, 88, 107, 204, 437, 443, 445, 455
    Calla lily, 41, 64, 119, 225, 401, 415, 439, 441, 447, 457, 475
    Easter lily, 171, 451
    Foxtail lily, 160, 451
    Gloriosa lily, 179, 211, 453, 455
    Lily of the valley, 52, 439
    Martagon hybrid, 226, 395, 457, 473
    Water lily, 362, 315, 465, 471
    Lily of the valley, 52, 439
Lisianthus, 56, 106, 287, 309, 348, 441, 445, 463, 465, 469
Lupine, 354, 469

M
Magnolia, 321, 467
Martagon hybrid, 226, 395, 457, 473
Mimosa, 191, 453
Muscari, 54, 373, 439, 471

N
Naples onion, 28, 437
Narcissus 48, 87, 170, 178, 192, 212, 408, 409, 439, 443, 451, 453, 455
Nerine, 32, 437
Nigella, 68, 140, 441, 449

O
Oncidium orchid, 81, 189, 200, 238, 352, 443, 453, 455, 459, 469
Orange chincherinchee, 218, 457
Orchid
    Cymbidium orchid, 286, 398, 463, 475
    Lady's slipper orchid, 174, 203, 389, 451, 455, 473
    James Story orchid, 239, 459
    Oncidium orchid, 81, 189, 200, 238, 352, 443, 453, 455, 459, 469
    Phalaenopsis orchid, 116, 447

P
Pansy, 99, 181, 445, 453
Paper white, 26, 437
Parrot tulip, 117, 341, 394, 447, 469, 473
Peony, 39, 70, 76, 77, 79, 123, 172, 176, 177, 281, 282, 288, 300, 305, 313, 318, 387, 390, 439, 441, 443, 447, 451, 453, 463, 465, 467, 473
Tree peony, 111, 249, 385, 445, 459, 473
Phalaenopsis orchid, 116, 447
Pincushion protea, 215, 455
Pitcher plant, 241, 400, 459, 475
Plum blossom, 320, 467
Plumosa celosia, 231, 391, 457, 473

Q
Queen Anne's lace, 157, 451
Quill, 266, 461
Quince, 72, 252, 254, 441, 459

R
Ranunculus, 23, 80, 114, 120, 152, 196, 206, 214, 217, 222, 243, 261, 274, 280, 289, 299, 307, 314, 319, 344, 410, 437, 443, 445, 447, 449, 455, 457, 459, 461, 463, 465, 467, 469, 475
    Butterfly ranunculus, 186, 453
    Ranunculus pom pom, 164, 451

Rose, 27, 36, 37, 51, 84, 85, 95, 100, 102, 105, 108, 109, 112, 115, 118, 122, 124, 126, 128, 161, 167, 175, 205, 221, 234, 250, 276, 278, 295, 296, 297, 301, 303, 306, 322, 339, 393, 437, 439, 443, 445, 447, 451, 455, 457, 459, 463, 465, 467, 469, 473

S

Scabiosa, 31, 137, 168, 317, 384, 414, 437, 449, 451, 467, 473, 475
Sedum, 324, 467
Sicilian onion, 155, 449
Snake's head fritillary, 165, 451
Snowball viburnum, 151, 449
Snowflake, 59, 441
Solomon's seal, 53, 439
Spider mum, 233, 237, 457, 459
Spirea, 34, 75, 437, 441
Spray carnation, 30, 38, 271, 388, 437, 439, 461, 473
Statice, 98, 138, 310, 445, 449, 465
Stock, 22, 89, 101, 437, 443, 445
Straw flower, 283, 463
Sunflower, 197, 405, 455, 475
Sweet pea, 58, 78, 135, 202, 242, 293, 298, 331, 340, 347, 353, 359, 441, 443, 447, 455, 459, 463, 465, 467, 469, 471
    Everlasting pea, 60, 441
Sweet William catchfly, 335, 467

T

Tree peony, 111, 249, 385, 390, 445, 459, 473
Tuberose, 132, 149, 447, 449
Tulip, 49, 63, 96, 117, 150, 153, 182, 184, 232, 263, 279, 308, 397, 403, 439, 441, 445, 447, 449, 453, 457, 461, 463, 465, 475
    French parrot tulip, 153, 187, 227, 270, 449, 453, 457, 461
    French tulip, 199, 455
    Parrot tulip, 341, 394, 469, 473
Tweedia, 19, 375, 437, 471

V

Veronica, 366, 471

W

Waratah, 302, 465
Water lily, 362, 315, 465, 471
Wax flower, 73, 162, 441, 451
Witch hazel, 188, 453

Y

Yarrow, 130, 194, 447, 453

Z

Zinnia, 253, 272, 328, 396, 459, 461, 467, 475

Flower Color Guide 플라워 컬러 가이드 확장 에디션

저자 테일러 & 마이클 퍼트남
역자 김정용
감수 이주희

2019년 11월 10일 초판 1쇄 발행
2021년 03월 02일 초판 2쇄 발행
2021년 12월 30일 중판 1쇄 발행
2025년 07월 01일 개정판 1쇄발행

펴낸곳 아트앤아트피플
펴낸이 송영희
디자인 이유리
마케팅 김철웅
인쇄 동아출판
출판등록 2015년 7월 10일 (제 315-2015-000048호)
주소 (우07535) 경기도 고양시 토당로 162번길 14 104동 802호
전화 070-7719-6967
팩스 02-6442-9046
홈페이지 http://www.artnartpeople.com
이메일 artnartpeoplekr@gmail.com

ISBN 979-11-90372-45-9

정가 46,000원